W7-CCG-939

BRUCE BUCHANAN is Assistant Professor of Government at the University of Texas at Austin, where he teaches courses on the presidency and public administration. His articles have appeared in a variety of public administration and political science journals.

The Presidential Experience

What the Office Does to the Man

Bruce Buchanan

A SPECTRUM BOOK

PRENTICE-HALL, INC., Englewood Cliffs, New Jersey 07632

Library of Congress Cataloging in Publication Data

Buchanan, Bruce.
   THE PRESIDENTIAL EXPERIENCE.

   (A Spectrum Book)
   Bibliography: p.
   Includes index.
   1. Presidents—United States. 2. Political
psychology. I. Title.
JK518.B83   353.03'13   78-16770
ISBN 0-13-697490-2
ISBN 0-13-697482-1 pbk.

B918

353.0313
B918

A Spectrum Book

10 9 8 7 6 5 4 3 2 1

Printed in the United States of America

PRENTICE-HALL INTERNATIONAL, INC., *London*
PRENTICE-HALL of AUSTRALIA PTY. LIMITED, *Sydney*
PRENTICE-HALL of CANADA, LTD., *Toronto*
PRENTICE-HALL of INDIA PRIVATE LIMITED, *New Delhi*
PRENTICE-HALL of JAPAN, INC., *Tokyo*
PRENTICE-HALL of SOUTHEAST ASIA PTE. LTD., *Singapore*
WHITEHALL BOOKS LIMITED, WELLINGTON, *New Zealand*

Contents

v

4

DEFERENCE:
The Impact of Status Inequality, 53

5

DISSONANCE:
The Lure of Expediency, 76

6

FRUSTRATION:
The Pressure to Prevail, 101

7

In Search
of the Philosopher-King, 125

8

THE PRESIDENTIAL EXPERIENCE:
Antidotes, 158

Many people provided major assistance at various stages in the development of this project. Professor Fred Greenstein of Princeton University and Professor James David Barber of Duke University offered important help and encouragement by reading and commenting upon early, shorter versions of the ideas in this book. Several colleagues in the Department of Government at the University of Texas at Austin helped me to shape my thinking early on. Professors James A. Bill, Neil R. Richardson, Neil Kotler, David Prindle, Karl Schmitt, and Gary Freeman each responded critically and constructively to one or another of the written products that emerged along the line. Others who read portions of the manuscript and offered useful suggestions were Neil Buchanan, Jack Corbett, and Stephanie Sokolewicz.

The book was conceived and developed in my graduate seminar on presidential behavior at the University of Texas at Austin. Members of that seminar did much to knock the rough edges off my thinking over the past four years. Too numerous to mention by name, I am nonetheless grateful to

Acknowledgments

them all. Professor Alan C. Elms of the University of California at Davis
saved me from more than one major error in judgement, and I regret the
circumstances that prevented my taking more of his excellent advice.

My greatest intellectual debt is to my colleague, Professor Jeff Millstone
of the Department of Government, University of Texas at Austin. From
beginning to end, Jeff offered patient, critical advice, forced me to clarify
my thinking, and helped me to sharpen my prose. His guidance and encouragement were instrumental in bringing this project to a conclusion. Finally, my thanks to the two women who swiftly and skillfully typed the
manuscript, Sue Aulds and Debbie Carey. None of the good people mentioned here can be held responsible for the flaws and omissions that remain.
Though much of any praise is deservedly theirs, the blame is mine alone.

Quotations from the book, *The Presidential Character,* 2nd Edition by James
David Barber. © 1977 by James David Barber. Published by Prentice-Hall,
Inc., Englewood Cliffs, N.J. 07632

Quote from "Carter Spins the World" is reprinted by permission from *Time*,
The Weekly Newsmagazine; Copyright Time Inc. 1977.

Brief Excerpt from *Kennedy* by Theodore C. Sorensen. Copyright © 1965 by
Theodore C. Sorensen. Reprinted by permission of Harper & Row, Publishers, Inc., and Hodder and Stoughton Ltd.

Specified exceprt from *Lyndon Johnson and the American Dream* by Doris
Kearns. Copyright © 1976 by Doris Kearns. Reprinted by permission of
Harper & Row, Publishers, Inc., and Andre Deutsch, Ltd.

Quotation from *A Thousand Days: John F. Kennedy in the White House* by
Arthur Schlesinger is used by permission of Houghton Mifflin Company and
Andre Deutsch, Ltd.

Quotation from *Nixon Agonistes* by Garry Wills. Copyright © 1969, 1970 by
Garry Wills. Reprinted by permission of Houghton Mifflin Company and Scott
Meredith Literary Agency, Inc.

Quotations reprinted from *The President: Office and Powers* by Edward S.
Corwin are used by permission of the publisher. © 1957 by New York University Press.

Quotations from *The Vantage Point* by Lyndon Baines Johnson. Copyright ©
1971 by HEC Public Affairs Foundation. Reprinted by permission of Holt,
Rinehart and Winston, Publishers.

Quotation from Harry S. Truman, *Memoirs*, vol. II, *Years of Trial and Hope,* Doubleday and Co., Inc., Publishers, 1955. Used by permission of Harry S. Truman Estate.

The influence of the office on the personality of its holder is, in fact, a fascinating study in the dynamics of political power.

LASKI, *The American Presidency*

People shape the roles and institutions in which they dwell. Conversely, institutions and roles are standardizing forces that exert enduring influences on the people who occupy them. These statements capture some essential features of reality. Few would seriously question the fundamental truth of either statement. Yet when it comes to the study of specific institutions and specific roles, one or the other of these directional assumptions tends to be dominant.

The presidency is a case in point. The presidency is both an institution and a role, studied primarily by political scientists and historians. When historians study the relationship between presidents and the presidency, they concentrate on how the first has shaped the second. Specifically, they focus on how individual presidents have contributed to the growth of presidential power.[1]

Similarly, political scientists tend to cast the president as the agent, the prime mover. The president acts; everything else reacts, including the presidential institution itself. In the hands of a forceful president, the presidency is a fulcrum, the great engine of the political system. He is the stimulus. The presidency, the political system, and the world, respond to his touch.[2]

Introduction

All this is, of course, true. But it tends to obscure the fact that the presidency, as an institution and as a role, has an impact of its own on the president as a person. To assert this is not to deny the reverse. It is simply to call attention to the fact that very little systematic attention has been given to the question of how the presidency influences presidents—in recurring and consequential ways.

This study is concerned with the impact of the presidency, as an institution and as a role, on presidents as human beings. I will try to make the following points.

First, there is an essential, trans-historical presidential experience, capable of influencing *any* incumbent, and tending to influence most of them in characteristic ways. The presidency confronts its incumbent with standardizing forces—a kind of presidential operant conditioning. The phrase "presidential experience" is intended to connote the collective sum of these forces, and to imply that they are commonly encountered by presidents-in-general.[3] I believe this to be true despite the variety and incomparability of historical situations and events that have confronted the various presidents, and despite the equally varied collection of personalities who have occupied the presidency. I further believe that certain facets of this core experience are discernible in the earliest presidencies, although my argument will be cast largely in the context of the modern era—Franklin Delano Roosevelt to the present.

Second, the origins of this common experience are essentially constitutional. It stems from the provision for a unitary executive, juxtaposed against competing legislative and judicial power centers, and augmented over the years by the sedimentary accretion of additional formal and informal functions and expectations for which the presidency is now held accountable. This means that neither the collective experience nor any of its components (identified below) can be eliminated or significantly altered on the initiative or at the discretion of a particular president. Changing the psychological force-field surrounding the presidency would require fundamental, constitutional changes in the functions and the very definition of the presidency.[4]

Third, the experience of concern is essentially *psychological*: a fourfold "environmental press" created and sustained by the role requirements of the presidency.[5] I will argue that the functions he performs give rise to certain characteristic exposures for the president as he goes about performing them. That is, the trans-historical continuity of the president's responsibilities gives rise to equally trans-historical consistencies and regularities in the kinds of psychologically important stimulation any president encounters in the course of his work.

Thus, I conceive the presidential experience as something whose origins are external (i.e., it originates outside the president's skull). Moreover, I believe that it is useful to conceive and describe the psychological pressure of the presidency independently of the perceptual idiosyncracies or response-propensities of any particular president.

This gives rise to a problem often encountered in political psychology: distinguishing the objective from the subjective environment.[6] Obviously, the psychological environment of the presidency cannot be described; indeed, it cannot even be said to exist—independently of the minds of presidents. There can be no psychological experience without psychologies to apprehend and undergo it. Thus it is impossible to describe the presidential experience without simultaneously being forced to incorporate assumptions about the perceptual and interpretive propensities of presidents. This creates a thorny problem, because behavior is influence by the environment as perceived and not by the so-called real environment (Greenstein, 1975). Consequently, different presidents may either perceive the same stimulus field in different ways or perceive different aspects of the same stimulus field; or they may even fail to perceive stimuli known to have been consequential for others.

How, then, a critic might ask, can it make any sense to argue that there is a common presidential experience, likely to shape attitudes and behavior in characteristic ways? Is not the "environmental press" you describe little more than your own reification of perceptions which you merely assume that presidents will experience, but which in fact may be experienced by only a few? At bottom, aren't there as many presidential experiences as there are presidents?

My answer will not satisfy epistemologists, but it comes down to this. I feel justified in referring to those facets of the presidential experience that I will bracket out for attention, as potentially influential psychological stimuli for three reasons:

1. The component pressures that make up the presidential experience can be shown to emerge from role demands that are grounded in brute realities independent of the perceiver.
2. The component pressures are analogous to classes of stimulation that have been shown, in social-psychological research, to be psychologically consequential for people in general, as represented by thousands of anonymous research subjects.
3. It is useful, for the presidency or any other job, to move beyond simple job descriptions into discussions of the characteristic kinds of psychological demands made by the job, if only as an heuristic device for evaluating the suitability of various candidates for the job. Thus, few would dispute the value of inquiring into the psychological demands made by jobs like Air Traffic Controller or Highway Patrolman.

These are the bases for my belief that it is reasonable to identify pressures and to characterize them as psychologically consequential for presidents in general, even though it might well be shown that they were of no consequence, had little impact, or perhaps didn't even *exist*, in the mind of any particular president.

Thus, I will rest what follows on the assumption that humans as a class share sufficient common susceptibilities to certain kinds of psychological influence to make it meaningful and, indeed, useful to search for and classify vectors of influence set in motion by the institutional circumstances of the presidency. Like any other job imbedded in any other institution, the presidency confronts its central figure with a fairly standard organization of circumstances. There are characteristic demands, cross-pressures, dilemmas, stresses, temptations, and supports which cannot be understood without reference to their psychological as well as their social, political, or historical meanings (Inkeles and Levinson, 1971, p. 432). I will try to show that these circumstances create vectors of influence which are recurring and consistent in kind, if not intensity, across presidencies. And I will argue that they are capable of working enduring impacts (socialization effects) on the attitudes and behavior of presidents in general because they recur, and because of the constancy of their direction vis-à-vis the person of the president.

Fourth, in reaching for a definition of the presidential experience, I have sought to reduce it to its basics. I believe that if one brackets out all that is nonessential, accidental, transitory, or ephemeral, one is left with four analytically discrete components which together comprise the fundamental and irreducible core or essence of that experience.[7] I will refer to these core components interchangeably as influence-vectors or pressures, that is, as constraining or compelling forces or influences. I have labeled these four pressures with words intended to connote their probable psychological meaning for presidents in general: stress, deference, dissonance, and frustration. Such words are often used to characterize the systematic psychological pressures encountered in a variety of common social and occupational situations, or manipulated in social-psychological research. This labeling is appropriate, for the pressures of the presidency are analogous in kind to those commonly experienced in any demanding occupation, though rarely in quite the same configuration. But the centrality of the presidency in this political system, as well as the unmatched visibility of the president, magnify their intensity quite beyond any normal experience.

The four points discussed thus far sketch, in broad outline, the substance of the argument to follow. Before proceeding, it will be helpful to acquaint the reader with some choices, aspirations, and values that have guided the preparation of this study.

First, it is already apparent that I have chosen to conceive and describe the presidential experience primarily in the language of the behavioral sciences, rather than in the language of history, or of the presidential institution itself. A brief example should clarify the distinction I am drawing. Instead of asking questions such as "How was Jackson influenced by being the symbol for his age?" or "How were presidents of the Cold War Era influenced by being Chiefs of State?", I will ask questions such as "How can the symbolic function, and the status inequality it inevitably produces (deference), be expected to influence the attitudes and behavior of the high status figure?"

Such language can seem bloodless and turgid, and it will offend the sensibilities of some readers. But it is useful for two reasons. It helps to focus attention on what is experientially common across presidencies and historical eras, rather than on what is unique or peculiar to them. And more important, such language encourages us to think of presidents as ordinary human beings, about whom generalizations might appropriately be drawn, rather than as Great Men, living symbols of the majesty of the republic, or as anthropomorphic embodiments of historical eras.[8] This makes it much easier to speak in general terms about how the job may work a long-run psychological impact on the people who hold it.

A second issue worth raising concerns the aspirations I have for this study. I conceive of this as the "So what?" question. What will be accomplished if I can argue plausibly that there is such a thing as a trans-historical presidential experience?

A study like this can help to clarify how and where, psychologically speaking, the presidency touches presidents—in recurring and consequential ways. The pressures point to those portions of the psychic anatomy likely to be engaged and tested by the job. This is useful information, I submit, for citizens and scholars who seek something more than casual or commonsensical answers to the question of who can (or who should) be president. This study enters an important gap in the presidential literature. For although prescriptive and analytic accounts of presidential character are numerous,[9] I have been unable to discover a single comprehensive treatment of the psychological environment of the presidency.[10] Yet before we can speak intelligently about who the president should be, we must learn more than we now know about what presidents have to be able to enjoy, tolerate—or, more grimly, to endure. A study of the presidency's characteristic psychological environment can shed clearer light on the kinds of personal resources needed to confront that environment on more or less equal terms. If it can be shown that the presidency confronts presidents with characteristic psychological demands, those demands can serve as *criteria* for assessing the general psychological suitability of candidates for the office. If we can systematize our understanding of what the presidency does to presidents, it will increase our ability to spot, in advance, personalities likely to experience the presidency either as an ordeal or as a transcendent opportunity for the expression of their greatest potential.

As the paragraphs that follow will show, I believe that the pressures are forceful and influential enough to threaten various aspects of the physical and mental functioning of any so-called "normal" healthy adult.[11] Coping with these pressures without succumbing to them is, I think, the central problem of the presidency from the point of view of the president.

A final prefatory comment. This study began as an examination of the psychological environment of the presidency rather than as an exercise in policy advocacy. My aim was to present my admittedly selective vision of what is and to call attention to some uses and implications of that vision for the presidency as it stands.

But my studies have led me to a value judgment—most apparent in Chapters 7 and 8—and best made plain at the outset. I believe that the presidency is dangerous—to the president, and to the stability of the political system. The job is dangerous to whoever holds it because it makes unmeetable demands on the personal resources of any single human being. I am convinced, for example, that under the right circumstances, the pressures are capable of doing the following things to anybody, regardless of the strength and quality of his character:

Straining physical and emotional resilience to the breaking point, (stress, Chapter 3 below).

Nurturing systematic distortions in the perceptions of the self and of external events, (deference, Chapter 4 below).

Eroding any values or scruples that interfere with the preservation of presidential power and dominance, including the canons of democracy, (frustration, Chapter 6 below).

Encouraging the use of secrecy, misrepresentation, and lying as weapons in the struggle for political success and survival (dissonance, Chapter 5 below).

Each of these consequences has posed serious threats to the stability of our political arrangements in the past.[12] Each is likely to do so again, unless steps are taken to lessen the impact of the presidential experience on presidents.

Of course it does make a difference who is president,[13] and I will consider some of the reasons in Chapter 7. Moreover, there is no simple cause and effect relationship between the pressures and political disaster. The presidential experience works its influence in subtle, gradual ways which accumulate over the long haul, whereas critical decisions or actions are usually galvanized by specific and immediate crises and events. But by influencing presidents in the ways described, the pressures increase the likelihood of dangerous responses to specific events. In this sense, they stand as latent threats to long-term political stability.

My analysis points clearly, I think, to the need for reform. We must find more reliable and more valid ways to spot both high quality presidential candidates *and* potentially disastrous candidates. We must also consider changes in the structure and procedures of the presidency if we are to minimize or arrest the dynamics of influence described in this book. Sterling character is necessary but is not sufficient as an antidote to the presidential experience—a point made in Chapter 7. Some changes that could help are considered in Chapter 8.

NOTES

1. See, for example, Schlesinger (1973); Cunliffe (1972); Burns (1965); Tugwell (1960); Hofstadter (1948); Small (1932).

2. Most textbooks and thematic essays on the presidency by political scientists view the president as a causal force. Cf. Cronin (1975); Hargrove (1974); Rossiter (1960). Neustadt appears to take a different view in observing that "[the president] needs to be an actor, yet he is preeminently a reactor, forced to be so by the nature of his work and its priorities (1969, p. 207)." However, his major work, *Presidential Power*, clearly casts the president as the independent variable.

3. The word "experience" has various usages. I will use the word in a

way that combines and extends two of the standard definitions, as given by *The American College Dictionary:* a) "the totality of the cognitions given by perception; all that is perceived, understood, and remembered." b) "to have experience of, meet with, undergo; feel." *synonym*: "implies being *affected* by what one meets with (pleasant or unpleasant), so that to a greater or lesser degree one suffers a change." Combining these definitions with appropriate modifications yields the meaning I will attribute to the word in these pages: "selective cognitions, made perceptible by repetition and force, and capable of *affecting* the perceiver's attitudes and/or behavior."

4. The interactive emphasis in political psychology holds that the chains of influence between actors and their environing institutions and roles are reciprocal; each influences the other. Cf. Greenstein (1975; 1973; 1969); Inkeles and Levinson (1971). Without denying that presidents leave their marks on the presidency, I will argue that certain features of the presidential role (namely, the functions performed by the president on behalf of the political system), have become so thoroughly imbedded in popular and scholarly conceptions of the presidency that it is idle to argue that a president could, at his own behest, simply disavow or ignore them. Although theoretically and technically possible, such behavior would surely provoke public outrage, and might well lead to impeachment proceedings or to a constitutional crisis. These functions are the source of the experience in question. Their uniformity and continuity from presidency to presidency underlies my claim that the experience they produce has a certain trans-historical consistency as well. Thus, presidents since George Washington have functioned as Chiefs of State, policy advocates, conflict mediators, and crisis managers, and have experienced the consequences of performing these functions.

5. The concept of "environmental press" is drawn from the theoretical writings of psychologist Henry A. Murray. The meaning ascribed to the concept in the test is best illustrated by the following excerpts from Hall and Lindzey's discussion of Murray's personology (1970; p. 180):

> Just as the concept of "need" represents the significant determinants of behavior within the person so the concept of "press" represents the *effective* or *significant* determinants of behavior in the environment [emphasis added]. . . . The press of [an environment] is what it can *do to the subject* or *for the subject*—the power that it has to affect the well-being of the subject in one

way or another. [emphasis in original]. . . . By representing the environment
in terms of *press* the investigator hopes to extract and classify the *significant*
portions of the world in which the individual lives [emphasis added]..

6. Though behavior is influenced by the environment as perceived, rather
than by the "real" environment, perceptions of reality have a grounding in brute events that are independent of the perceiver (Greenstein,
1975; p. 6). The functions presidents must perform give rise to characteristic kinds of exposures. For example, because presidents are both
symbols and political advocates, they get treated in characteristic ways
by various groups (e.g., with unusual respect by most citizens, with a
certain guarded suspicion by most members of Congress, and with
thinly veiled mistrust by much of the working press). Or, because
presidents are crisis managers, certain kinds of problems that arise are
always the president's problem (he and not someone else must cope
with any sudden national emergency). These are the kinds of "brute
events" which produce characteristic and recurring exposures for any
president. And it is reasonable to assume not only that such events will
be perceived, but that repeated exposure to them may be psychologically influential. Moreover, the subject may be influenced, yet may
remain consciously unaware of it. See the discussions of deference and
dissonance in Chapter 1. Such instances require an external analyst to
perceive and assay the extent of influence.

7. The language of this paragraph is borrowed from phenomenology, a
conceptual stance which stresses the careful description of
phenomena, as distinct from ontological or epistemological questions
(see Schutz, 1967; Berger and Luckman, 1967). It is unnecessary to
embrace this perspective specifically, but the language helps to clarify
the aims of this study. Paraphrasing R. P. Hummel, phenomenology
in this context refers to nothing more than a technique for reducing
[the] experience of life in [the presidency] to its basics. Phenomenology is an analytical method that brackets out from our experience all
that is accidental and unessential. After such an analysis is applied to
[the presidency] we are left with what fundamentally makes up the
[presidential] experience—those characteristics without which life in
[the presidency] would not be life in [the presidency]. (1977; p. 34).

8. The following excerpt from Stephen B. Oates's biography of Lincoln
suggests the kind of language I have sought to avoid, and something of
why I have sought to avoid it:

He comes to us in the mists of legend as a homespun "rail-splitter" from the Illinois prairies, a saintly commoner who called himself "Abe," spoke in a deep, fatherly voice, and cared little about material rewards and social station. He also comes to us as Father Abraham, the Great Emancipator who led the North off to civil war to free the slaves and after the conflict ended offered the South a tender and forgiving hand. That is the Lincoln of mythology and the folk-hero of the legend-building histories, but it is not the Lincoln who actually lived" (1977; p. xv).

Though inappropriate here, such language has its uses. Oates attributes much of Lincoln's political ideology, particularly his steadfast devotion to the principles of union, to the fact that he had read and been inspired by Weemsian and other romanticized accounts of the men and issues of the Federalist Era.

9. Recent discussions of character traits presidents should possess can be found in Hargrove (1974); Hess (1974); and Hughes (1972). Characterological schemes for classifying presidents include Barber (1977) and Hargrove (1966). In addition, a number of "psychobiographies" have appeared recently. Among them: Barber (1977); Brodie (1974); Clinch (1973); Kearns (1976); Mazlish (1972) and Rogan (1975).

10. For the most part, available treatments of the president's work environment are institutional and descriptive accounts of his duties and the various constituencies with whom he must interact (See Cronin 1975; Koening, 1975; Hargrove, 1974; Rossiter, 1960). In these and other notable works, attention to the psychological dimensions of the job is impressionistic and sporadic. For example, David Truman asserts, without further elaboration, that "both its prominence and its symbolic functions make the presidential office a more important molder of its incumbents than any other in the nation, possibly excepting only the Supreme Court. To enter upon the presidency is to alter the whole fabric of one's accustomed relationships" (1951; p. 400). Richard Neustadt (1969) speaks of "dilemmas" being the president's "daily bread." He, like Cronin (1975; p. 238), attribute such dilemmas to a gap between unrealistic public expectations and the president's capacity to deliver. Both imply that this situation has psychological consequences for the president, but neither elaborates. Another widespread theme in the literature is the burden and strain imposed on the president by his job. For example, David Coyle (1960) characterizes the presidency as an "ordeal" for the president, and describes the pain and suffering of presidents from Washington through FDR, but without benefit of any systematic psychological conception of the sources of

that pain. Similar accounts of presidential suffering can be found in Tugwell (1960) and Binkley (1958). Tugwell writes:

All of them [presidents of the Federalist era] were, before long, unhappy and harrassed. Only a few found themselves possessed of the talents for so complex and demanding a job, and as a consequence a feeling of inadequacy soon succeeded the euphoria of victory; and the Mansion. . .became a place of strain and sadness. . . . There have been exceptions, but the procession of the Presidents must be said to be a sequence of aging and weighed-down men struggling against disrupting influences, conscious of carrying almost alone national responsibilities, and constantly discouraged that so much that ought to be done could not be accomplished (1960; p. 84).

Binkley devotes a chapter of his 1958 book to the "Pressures on the President," by which he means the episodic emergence of sudden demands for which the president is accountable. As in Tugwell's book, psychological pressure is implied but not described in specific terms (1958, p. 41–63). Finally, several explicitly psychological treatments of various aspects of the presidential work environment have recently appeared. Barber's (1977) schema embodies two environmental variables of psychological import: the "power situation" and the "climate of expectations." These differ from the approach taken in the present study because the concepts require temporal specification in terms of particular presidencies or historical eras in order to be meaningful. That is, it makes little sense to speak of the "power situation" or the "climate of expectations" as trans-historically consistent, while terms like "frustration" or "deference" can have meaning independently of historical context. Irving Janis's study, *Victims of Group-Think* (1972) applies social-psychological perspectives on group dynamics to an analysis of presidential decisions under stressful conditions. George Reedy's *The Twilight of the Presidency* (1970) is expressly concerned with some psychological consequences of isolating and deferring to presidents. Both Janis and Reedy offer important insights which are incorporated here, particularly in the analysis of the *deference* experience. But neither work aspires to comprehensiveness, hence both omit attention to other important psychological forces at play in the president's workplace.

11. I have no wish to enter into the debate about what constitutes "normality" in human beings. My use of the word "normal" here is intended only to suggest that one need not be psychopathic, mentally unbalanced, or paranoid to be influenced in what I believe are harmful and undesirable ways by the demands of the presidency.

12. On the question of physical and emotional strain in office, see Milton Plesur, "The Health of Presidents," in Tugwell and Cronin (1974). Plesur concludes that ". . .though generalizations on the basis of only 35 deceased men are tenuous, it is true that the average duration of Presidential life has been shorter than might have been expected. . . .Added to pomp and circumstances as a never-ending source of tension are physical fatigue and emotional drain. No responsible union would ever approve the President's hours of work for a "hard-hat"; and an insurance company would probably define the ordinary White House occupant as a poor insurance risk!" (p. 189). Among the presidents displaying marked physical or emotional strain, which, in context, posed threats to political stability is Woodrow Wilson, whose illness following upon the League of Nations dispute so incapacitated him that his wife assumed his duties, causing widespread uneasiness (Weinstein, 1967). Others include Eisenhower, Lyndon Johnson, and Richard Nixon. Concerning distorted presidential perceptions and resultant ill-conceived decisions which I will attribute to the conditioning of deference, the case of Nixon's dismissal of Archibald Cox as Special Watergate Prosecutor is instructive. Regarding the ascendancy of presidential power over democratic values, interpretations of specific incidents depend heavily on the values of the interpreter. But the record is peppered with legalistic disputes over the constitutional prerogatives of the president, which points up recurring fears that the presidency threatens democratic values (Corwin, 1957). And few would dispute that the traditions of the presidency, plus the judgments of historians concerning presidential greatness, stand as inducements for presidents to identify with an aggressive model of the presidency (see Bailey, 1966). This model is represented by such diverse interpretations as Corwin's "strong" president, Burns's "Hamiltonian " and "Jeffersonian" models, Theodore Roosevelt's "Stewardship" theory, FDR's "expansionist" presidency, Richard Neustadt's essentially amoral primer on presidential power, and Richard Nixon's bald assertion that "if the president orders it, it is not illegal" (television interview with David Frost, May 19, 1977). I will argue that behavior consistent with these views is encouraged by the frustration attending the inevitable opposition that gathers around any presidential initiative. The history of the presidency clearly reveals the existence of an ideology that ennobles presidential power as good unto itself. This ideology justifies, and thus encourages aggressive responses to frustration in any president, though of course not all succumb to it. Secrecy and

lying are widely viewed as essential resources by political professionals, and few students would deny that circumstances arise in which they are genuinely necessary. But threats to political stability emerge when such behavior is exposed, and, as in the case of Nixon and Watergate, call not only the integrity of the president into question, but also the very legitimacy of the presidential institution itself.

13. James David Barber (1977) makes this point convincingly, and in terms that can be understood by anyone. My contention is not that character is irrelevant but that it is not enough, for a variety of reasons, to shield against dangerous presidential behavior in perpetuity. The pressures of the presidency are such that even the most suitable of characters will occasionally be provoked into error. Suitable characters will tend, on the balance, to behave suitably, but they still might, in uncharacteristic moments, take action that threatens the identity or the stability of the political system. For example, FDR's attempt to change the Supreme Court, John Kennedy's handling of the Cuban Missile Crisis, and Gerald Ford's pardon of Richard Nixon all did violence to values that I cherish. Respectively, these decisions might well have (but did not) produced a fundamental change in the nature of our government, led to a nuclear war with Russia, or permanently undermined the legitimacy of the presidency in the eyes of American citizens. Yet Barber classifies each of these men as Active-Positives, those temperamentally best equipped to govern. (I agree with his classifications.) Thus, character offers no *secure* solution to the problem, even if, as many argue, it remains the only realistic solution. It only takes one slip to open the floodgates. And some future president, at some point, seems destined to make that slip.

. . . Whereas "legislative power" and "judicial power" denote fairly definable functions *of government as well as fairly constant* methods *for their discharge, "executive power" is still indefinite as to* function *and retains, particularly when it is exercized by a single individual, much of its original plasticity as to* method. *It is consequently the power of government that is the most spontaneously responsive to emergency conditions; conditions, that is, which have not attained enough of stability or recurrency to admit of their being dealt with according to rule.*

CORWIN, *The President: Office and Powers 1787–1957*

In one sense the functions of the presidency *are* indefinite: They assume specific, substantive definition only as previously unencountered national problems arise and become part of the president's portfolio in his capacity as chief troubleshooter. In another, more generic, sense, however, the functions of the presidency have been discernible since the earliest presidencies. The power of the office has increased dramatically with the scope of its activities, but the

ORIGINS:
The Generic
Functions
Of the Presidency

underlying responsibilities for representing, maintaining, managing, and protecting the national political order have inhered in the presidency since the time of Washington.

In this short chapter I want to distinguish between the *generic functions* of the presidency, which are few in number, and the far more numerous "hats" or "chiefships" the president has accumulated in the process of performing his generic functions.

His generic functions arise from his fundamental responsibility to the polity: system maintenance and survival.[1] His various chiefships identify the specific, substantive details of his work. Many of the latter are relatively recent additions to the president's portfolio.[2] His generic functions, however, have been trans-historically consistent.

Thus, presidents have functioned as symbols since the earliest days of the first Washington administration, despite the fact that views of what constitutes effective symbolic behavior on the part of presidents have varied dramatically since then.[3] Similarly, presidents have functioned as partisan policy advocates ever since an embittered George Washington abandoned his nonpartisan stance in his second term and began openly espousing Federalist doctrines. Because the country needed a sense of direction and the Congress was then, as now, unable to muster a consensus, the president emerged as the most visible and influential advocate of national priorities and has remained such ever since, despite lulls in influence and changes in methodology.[4]

Because the nation is geographically vast and dispersed, it has always suffered from threats to its internal harmony and stability posed by the conflicts between diverse social, economic, and political interests. The presidency, with its national electoral base and symbolic prominence, has always functioned as a mediator between such interests. Washington sought to perform this function through the instrument of the cabinet, then a bipartisan collection of Northern mercantile and Southwestern agrarian interests, led in order by Hamilton and Jefferson. Though the cabinet would later lose its representative character, presidents would continue to function as focal points and safety valves. The issues and the groups have varied; presidential tools, methods, and techniques have changed. But the underlying presidential mandate vis-à-vis contending interests has stayed the same: Find a way to defuse passions and reduce conflict before they explode and threaten to undermine the social fabric.

Finally, national emergencies, both internal and external, have always been the president's problem. The kinds of emergencies have varied. Their magnitude and their international significance have increased geometrically over time. Value conflicts over the appropriate use of presidential power in crisis situations have arisen and been disputed throughout the country's history. Presidential interpretations of this function, and presidential strategies for performing it, have varied from administration to administration, from crisis to crisis. In spite of such changes, the primary responsibility for internal and external crisis management has rested, throughout American history, with the presidency.

Symbol, policy advocate, mediator, and crisis manager, then, are the core functions—the things presidents have been enjoined to do in the process of meeting the fundamental responsibility for maintaining the political system in the face of uncertainty. Omitted from this reckoning are the many specific duties—the sediment of past encounters with national problems—which for present purposes can be subsumed under the broader generic categories.

To stress the historical continuity of the core functions is not to deny that presidents have attended to them with varying emphases and methods. Nor do I mean to trivialize the vastness and importance of changes that have taken place. The stage on which the president moves has expanded tremendously with the rise of the United States as a world power. Nuclear technology, electronic communications, and jet air travel have each produced fundamental changes in the methods and powers of presidents, as well as in their centrality and visibility. My argument is simply that the historical consistency of the president's responsibilities produces a like consistency in the kinds of exposures he will encounter as he goes about the business of performing his functions. Dramatic increases in power, in visibility, and in specific duties have obviously multiplied and intensified his exposures. But I do not believe that these changes have altered either the qualitative nature of such exposures or the kinds of psychological influence they are likely to exert.

Thus, although Jimmy Carter reaches and seeks to inspire the people by means of electronic media, George Washington was no less a symbol for touring the nation in a horse-drawn coach. And as symbols, both were constantly exposed to deferential treatment by those around them. John Quincy Adams unsuccessfully advocated the construction of highways and canals; Franklin Roosevelt sought to alter the composition of the Supreme Court: Both were advocating policies they deemed important to the national interest, and both were frustrated in their aims by concerted opposition. Kennedy confronted Russian missiles; Lincoln faced Confederate armies: Each was coping with a crisis that threatened the survival of the society, and each experienced considerable stress in the process. Washington sought to reconcile the schism between Jeffersonian Republicans and Hamiltonian Federalists; Truman sought the common ground between labor unions and industrialists: Each was working to defuse latent threats to domestic tranquility. And each was anxious about the explosiveness of his situation and the uncertainty of its outcome.

If we are to clarify the regularities inherent in the presidential experience, we must depart from an appreciation for the underlying, trans-historical stability of the president's *functions* in the political system. Each of his responsibilities—symbol, mediator, advocate, and crisis manager—virtually guarantees recurring and consistent kinds of personal exposures for the president. These are the brute realities with which he must contend. As we shall see, their influence potential stems from the facts of repetition and force, and from the consistency of direction with which they bear upon the president. As a symbol, the president is repeatedly exposed to deferential, celebratory treatment. As mediator and crisis manager, he is routinely beset by stressful demands which tax his physical and psychological resources. As policy advocate, he attracts controversy like a magnet, and is thus repeatedly exposed to determined political opposition. And as his troubles mount, and he discovers the considerable moral leeway available to presidents, he will inevitably feel the temptation to fall back on the expedient manipulation of information and the strategic use of secrecy as a political resource in the service of his power stakes. Each of these exposures can, in time, *condition* the president's attitudes and canalize his behavior, as the following chapters on various pressures will attempt to show.

With this preliminary sense of how his job shapes his experience, we turn in Chapter 2 to a more systematic consideration of how the functions intermingle to standardize the exposures and routinize the influences to which presidents are subjected.

NOTES

1. There is a large body of theoretical literature on leadership and management which adopts a generic view of the functions of executives in general, and which converges on the view that the essential function is system maintenance and survival in the face of unprogrammed problems. For example, Chester Barnard (1938) asserts that executive work is not the work of the organization, but the specialized work of maintaining the organization in operation. He identifies three maintenance functions: (1) providing the system of communication, (2) securing essential efforts from subordinate agents, and (3) the formulation and definition of purpose. In *Leadership in Administration* (1957), Phillip Selznick identifies four generic tasks: (1) definition of institutional mission and role, (2) institutional embodiment of purpose (creating administrative machinery), (3) defense of institutional integrity, and (4) the ordering of internal conflict. Similarly, Katz and Kahn, in their *Social Psychology of Organizations* (1966), emphasize the maintenance function of top management, particularly the responsibility for anticipating and responding to a turbulent and unpredictable external milieu, without altering the basic character of the enterprise in the process of adaptation. More recently, generic conceptions of *presidential* functions similar to that offered here have appeared. Richard Tanner Johnson, (1974, p. xvi; xxi), for example, speaks of "conflict" between the president's political and managerial roles, and argues:

The President's prime managerial concern becomes one of integrating—or drawing together—these divergent organizational units and imbuing them with the administration's goals and priorities. . . .The President's public role establishes a subtle but important distinction between the President of the United States and the chief executives of lesser enterprises. He has, in effect, the means at his disposal to reach beyond the immediate boundaries of his organization to create new resources. . . . He has an unparalleled legitimacy. In a sense he commands not only the Executive branch but its environment! He can go to the people. . . . In the face of many constraints, the President can work on the system [the executive branch] from without and from within.

In a departure from customary textbook practices, Cronin (1975, p. 251) identifies six generic functions—symbolic leadership, priority setting and program design, crisis management, legislative and political coalition-building, program implementation and evaluation "follow-through," and oversight of government routines—performed across three policy domains, (foreign policy, aggregate economics, and domestic polity). Similar in spirit is Haider (1976, p. 14), who, in "Management and the Presidency: From Preparation to Performance," asserts that, "a Chief Executive has the difficult tasks of information gathering, viewing partisan benefit and the public interest, knowing limits of resources and government capabilities, and weighing alternatives. These tasks are both subtle and sensitive. They are also managerial in nature." One scholar who has recently taken issue with the view of the president as manager still embraces the generic stance:

> My contention is that Presidents have made a serious mistake, starting with [Franklin] Roosevelt, in asserting that they are the chief managers of the federal government. . . . "Rather than chief manager, the President is chief political officer of the United States. His major responsibility, in my judgment, is to annually make a relatively small number of highly significant political decisions—among them, setting national priorities, which he does through the budget and his legislative proposals, and devising policy to ensure the security of the country, with special attention to those situations that could involve the nation in war (Hess, 1976, p.11).

Though varying in emphasis and complexity, these selections illustrate what is meant here by generic functions. For contrast with the "duty" perspective on the job, characteristic of presidency textbooks, see footnote #2.

2. Perhaps the best-known list of presidential "chiefships" is Clinton Rossiter's (1960, p. 1–33), which identifies five as expressly constitutional, and five more as evolving from the exigencies of national experience. The first group: Chief of State, Chief Executive, Commander-in-Chief, Chief Diplomat, and Chief Legislator. The second: Chief of Party, Voice of the People, Manager of Prosperity, World Leader, and Protector of the Peace. Similar lists appear in Koenig (1975) and in Sidney Hyman's article, "What Makes a 'Strong' President?" *New York Times Magazine*, December 13, 1953, which identifies no less than fifteen chiefships. Updated lists of this kind would have to include Chief Protector of Energy Resources, the latest of the problems to land on the president's desk.

3. A symbol is a material object representing something immaterial. As the dominant symbol of government, the president represents the values, majesty, integrity, and potency of the political system. When effective, his symbolic behavior elicits respect, support, and compliance from citizens. To citizens for whom it is credible, it provides inspiration, reassurance, and a sense of legitimacy. His symbolic responsibilities were of great concern to Washington, who sought by every word and deed to reinforce the fragile legitimacy of the fledgling republic (see J.T. Flexner, *Washington: The Indispensible Man*, 1970). Washington was roundly criticized for his royalist deportment, and Thomas Jefferson was to exploit this sentiment by de-emphasizing all vestiges of royalty and majesty, dressing shabbily, walking freely among the people, and generally styling himself as "first citizen" rather than monarch. The contrast is similar to that between Richard Nixon, who identified with the majestic presidency, and first citizen Jimmy Carter, who, like Jefferson, sought to reduce the status gap between president and citizens.

4. The primacy of the presidency with respect to this function has, of course, varied, with Congress periodically reasserting itself and seizing the initiative (see Burns, 1965; Schlesinger, 1973). Also, methods have varied, particularly following upon demonstrations, first by Jefferson, later by Jackson, that political parties were an effective means of routinizing both legislative and mass political support (see Young, *The Washington Community*, 1966, and Schlesinger, *The Age of Jackson*, 1945.)

. . . Certain personality theorists have centered their theoretical position about the importance of the psychological environment *or the subjective frame of reference. This is a matter of emphasizing that the physical world and its events can affect the individual only as he perceives or experiences them. Thus, it is not objective reality which serves as a determinant of behavior but rather objective reality as it is* perceived *or assigned meaning by the individual. It is the psychological environment, not the physical environment, which determines the manner in which the individual will respond.*

HALL AND LINDZEY, *Theories of Personality*

We must concede the essential subjectivity of anything so personal as a psychological environment. But we might still reasonably expect that any regularities in the "real" environment may produce concomitant regularities in that which is subjectively perceived. At the very least, patterns in the real environment will result in patterns of exposure, whether he who is exposed perceives them or not.

The brute realities of the president's environment are the

SETTING:
The Psychological
Environment
Of the Presidency

2

functions he must perform. Presidents routinely discover that, whatever their personal priorities, the environment demands that they allocate their energies according to the emergent needs of the polity. The environment delivers the agenda and compels attention to the agenda as delivered. Presidents routinely discover that self-determination is a rarity and a luxury. If his functions produce recurring and characteristic exposures for the president, then it is possible and certainly useful to try to classify those exposures and to assess their potential for influencing attitudes and behavior. Do the bits and pieces of his daily experience sort themselves into something like a causal texture? Can his exposures be represented as consistent vectors of influence, with canalizing impacts on attitudes and behavior? Yes.

Figure 1 identifies the exposures presidents encounter in the process of performing their functions. As noted in the Introduction, the exposures are conceived as pressures—constraining or compelling forces or influences. They are labeled stress, deference, dissonance, and frustration. I believe that these four pressures capture the psychologically important exposures that presidents repeatedly undergo, and represent the shortest list that can be drawn up without omitting something important. And I have labeled them with words that suggest their probable psychological meaning for presidents in general.

Exposure to *stress* is an inevitable consequence of the mediator and crisis management functions. These functions impart a turbulence, an unpredictability, an episodic intensity, and a bewildering variety to any president's work experience. The term "stress" is intended to connote the fact that most presidents find these features of

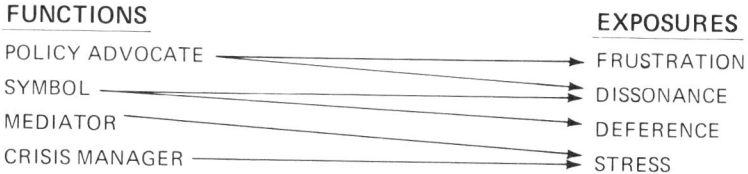

Figure 1 Recurring Exposures that Result from Performing the Functions of the Presidency

the job to be physically wearing and emotionally draining, though a hardy few have experienced them as thoroughly exhilarating.

Exposure to *deference* is an unavoidable consequence of the symbolic function. The word "deference" captures an essential and recurring quality of any president's face-to-face encounters with other people. Presidents are the only Americans routinely treated with special awe and exaggerated respect by anyone they meet personally. Much of this treatment is explicitly ceremonial and rather perfunctory. Some of it is spontaneous, subtle, and implicit. Though responses to deference will vary, few human beings can remain impervious to such comprehensive and systematically distorted treatment for the four or eight years of a presidential term.

Dissonance arises from a conjunction of the symbolic and policy advocate functions. An awkward term, used for want of a better word, "dissonance" implies that presidents, as symbols and advocates, are encouraged to misrepresent themselves to their various constituencies: in the first instance to inspire, in the second to *persuade*. Things are rarely quite what they seem, and presidents must, if they are to be effective as symbols or as advocates, cast things in the best possible light. Thus, they routinely conceal any personal facts that would, if revealed, seem inconsistent with their symbolic stature. And they tend just as routinely to trumpet whatever interpretation of events seems most likely to help them win acceptance for their priorities. The recurring exposure is temptation, for the circumstances of the presidency invite the use of lying or dissembling as an expedient political resource. His unusual moral freedom encourages him to depend more and more heavily on this resource as his troubles accumulate. As far as we know, some few presidents have totally resisted this temptation. A great many have not.[1]

Frustration is the product of the policy advocate function, and it describes the classic experience of democratic political leadership. Whatever he advocates, any president can expect to meet stiff and concerted opposition to his plans. Because other legitimate formal and informal power centers are capable of thwarting him, he will be thwarted—in small *and* large ways—throughout his tenure. The greater his policy ambitions, the more frequent will be his exposure to opposition, and the more recurrent his feelings of frustration and irritation. Reactions to such experience have varied, but every president must cope with it.

These are the vectors of influence set in motion by performing the functions of the presidency: abstractions of the significant psychological press that characterizes the president's job environment.[2]

In successive chapters I analyze each pressure in detail, illustrate its operation with examples drawn from the recent and distant history of the presidency, and discuss its probable impacts on attitudes and behavior.

In the remainder of this chapter I want to expand upon the skeletal conception of the president's work environment drawn thus far. Some elaboration will help to illuminate the nature of the psychological environment and its probable meaning for presidents. And it should serve to clarify the dynamics of its operation.

First, it is important to realize that the president's job is not all burden, pain, and strain. Though he is surrounded by forceful and influential stimulation of varying kinds, much of it is subtle and only vaguely perceptible (dissonance), or even flattering and enjoyable (deference). Stress and frustration are burdensome for the most part. But the president need not be suffering in order to be influenced by even these less pleasant aspects of his job. The history books overflow with accounts of presidential agony (see Introduction Note 10). But it is a mistake to assume that pain is the only, or even the most important, consequence for the presidential person. For all of its burdens, there has never been a shortage of candidates for the position. Moreover, some measure of stress and frustration can be challenging, invigorating, even essential to human development.

Second, it is necessary to emphasize that the pressures derive their influence potential from *repetition*. It is a psychological truism that a recurring stimulus eventually produces a conditioned response in animal or human organisms (Pavlov, 1927; Skinner, 1938). Similarly, it is argued here that cumulative exposures to stress, deference, dissonance, and frustration will eventually condition the perceptions and responses of presidents. This is not to suggest that immediate circumstances or situations can have no influence without repetition. They can. It is only to emphasize that the concern here is with how the regularities of his experience are likely to influence the president over time.

More can be said of the relation between the pressures and presidential behavior. From the emphasis just placed on the importance of repetition, it is apparent that no direct or straightforward isomorphism between stimulus and response is presumed. In fact, there is evidence which suggests that people respond or conform to only about one-half of the social inputs to which they are exposed (Barker and Wright, 1955). Ecological psychologists contend that the influence of environmental forces on behavior become apparent over long, rather than short, segments of the behavioral stream (Barker, 1965). Thus, presidential experience and behavior cannot, for the most part, be expected to occur in causally coupled units. One scholar has advanced a conception of environmental influence that helps to make this point (Shoggen, 1963). Shoggen conceives of an *Environmental Force Unit* (EFU) as an action by an environmental agent toward a recognizable end-state for a person. EFUs involve series, or programs, of discrete inputs. And the unity of an EFU derives from the constancy of direction of its component inputs, with respect to the person on whom it bears. Shoggen argues that a person's behavior is more frequently responsive to or consistent with intact EFUs than with separate incidents within a given EFU.

Thus, we might conceive of stress, deference, dissonance, and frustration as environmental force units, consistent in direction, though manifesting themselves episodically and intermittntly throughout a president's term, and conducive to attitudinal and behavioral end-states as exposures accumulate. For example, the recognizable end-state of recurring presidential exposure to deference might be an artificially inflated self-concept and a concomitant tendency to overestimate the impact that one can have on external events. But for the most part, we would not expect any given exposure to deferential treatment (e.g., an aide's fulsome praise of the

President's State of the Union address) to result in abrupt psychological or behavioral responses. Similar reasoning can be applied to each of the other pressures.

Finally, mention should be made of the probable mind-set of a president in office—a predisposition which, I think, colors all of his sensations and heightens his susceptibilities to influence throughout his term of office.[3] Presidents will, of course, differ in this and other ways. But such differences are reserved for discussion in Chapter 7, which takes up the question of presidential character. Here the focus is on those common psychological predispositions that serve to enhance susceptibility to the pressures of the job.

It is obvious, for example, that the process of seeking and winning the presidency involves a heavy psycho-emotional investment of the self.[4] Except for those rare instances where the president-elect or president-designate has been reluctant to serve, or has been surprised by sudden elevation to office (e.g., Washington, Truman, Ford), the president-elect has labored and schemed against improbable odds for years before capturing the prize. In all probability, he has given long and searching thought not only to his prospects for election, but to his suitability for office, to the kind of president he would try to be, and to whether he could be equal to the difficulties he knows he would encounter. He has summoned his resolve and made a decision to stay the course. He has publicly avowed his position on a host of topical, controversial issues, contested and debated these positions in front of the nation, and finally, he has been vindicated at the polls in what must stand as the most exhilarating, massively reinforcing, and beholding, of *rites de passage* (Van Gennep, 1960). Promises have been made and the mantle bestowed. Now the president must deliver.

This gives rise to what I believe is the central common predisposition of presidents in office: the feeling of *responsibility*.[5] Presidential biographies concur that the euphoria of election triumph soon gives way to a sober appreciation for the enormity of the task at hand and for the inexorable accountability of the president for all that transpires thereafter.[6] Responsibility is certainly the burden most frequently mentioned in the writings of former presidents, and apparently it has been seen as the sensation most joyfully dispensed with at the close of numerous presidential terms.[7]

The importance of this feeling is that it invests everything that happens to him or around him with the power to confirm or deny his self-definition. And his milieu is turbulent and unpredictable. He has staked his sense of worth, his claim to political support, and his right to a place in history on an assumption that must be proved again and again: that he can be equal to any difficulty that might arise.

The president, like any other careerist, sees his work as an extension of his identity. Through his work, he *implements* his self-concept.[8] He is ego-involved. Work is the area in which he strives to validate his identity and the competencies it embraces.

But unlike most other careerists, he must play for keeps under conditions of great uncertainty, incomplete information, severe time limits, and near-total visibility. He is uniquely vulnerable, and there is no place to hide.

With such a tremendous investment of identity at stake, it becomes clear that recurring exposures to stress, deference, dissonance, and frustration constitute exposures to *self-relevant* stimulation. Stress is stress not only because it exhausts physical and emotional energies, but because it may threaten the validity of the self-concept. The possibility of important failure is always present, hence the president's reputation is on the line. Should a sudden crisis result in embarrassment or disaster for the United States, the president's stature will suffer, not only in the eyes of citizens, but even more painfully, in his own eyes. Conversely, deference, whatever its other consequences, is a ubiquitous reminder that one has achieved a station in life that is estimable in its own right, regardless of the ebbs and flows of the political wars. Thus, it can capture the president's attention, and may even turn his head, if only because it is a small but dependable source of confirmation in a milieu that repeatedly threatens to disconfirm his pretensions. Dissonance is tempting, in part because so often in presidential history, misrepresentation has been the only or the most expedient way either to save the presidential face or to orchestrate a resounding triumph not readily accomplished by conventional means.[9] And frustration—the thwarting of presidential initiative—is the ultimate threat to his public and his private stature. To varying degrees, presidents will be motivated to circumvent and prevail over opposition, if only because all of them are aware that history rewards those who succeed, not those who allow themselves to be outmaneuvered.[10]

In this chapter we have necessarily adopted a broad, skeletal view of the president's psychological environment. The aim has been to suggest how characteristic exposures (pressures) emerge from performing the generic functions of the role, to stress the gradual and cumulative nature of their influence, and to argue that because the president is ego-involved, such exposures can hardly fail to affect him in various ways.

The next four chapters look closely and carefully at each of the pressures in turn. Following definitions and illustrations, the focal question in each chapter is: How can this pressure be expected to influence presidential attitudes and behavior? I start with stress: that aspect of the job which more than any other justifies the popular conception of the presidency as the toughest job in America.

NOTES

1. Presidential "lying" varies dramatically in nature and in its consequences for the polity. Much of it can be seen merely as the strategic control of information, withheld or misrepresented for the legitimate purpose of preserving decisional options, as when John Kennedy fabricated an illness in order to buy time to formulate a response to the presence of Russian missiles in Cuba. Misrepresentations like this seem in themselves relatively inconsequential, and are widely accepted as necessary. Less easily dismissed are the distortions and deprecations undertaken for the purpose of discrediting opposition or advancing policy objectives. I have in mind here the kind of cynicism captured in Thomas Cronin's (1975, p. 148) "Presidency Public Relations Script" admonition: "Claim Credit When Things Go Right and Decentralize Blame! Choose Problems For Their Potential Credit

Value!'' Or the use of secrecy as a means of avoiding the need to obtain democratic sanction for presidential initiatives, such as the secret bombing of Cambodia, or John and Robert Kennedy's alleged use of the Mafia to attempt the assassination of Fidel Castro. Seemingly most damaging are those instances where the president lies for what are later revealed to be motives of self-interest or personal protection, as with Nixon's pronouncements in the Watergate affair. The national reaction to this event suggests that such acts undermine the legitimacy of the presidency, and not just the president, in the public's eyes. They thus threaten to weaken support for and identification with governmental institutions. See Chapter 4.

2. It is worth noting that the frequency and intensity of these exposures will vary across presidencies in accordance with such factors as: (1) the policy ambitions of the president; (2) the nature and extent of international tensions prevalent at the time; (3) the domestic climate of expectations; (4) the domestic power situation and the intensities of the conflicts it embodies at any given time; and (5) the characterological predilections of particular presidents. On this last point, see Chapter 7.

3. A "mind-set" can be defined as a predisposition to perceive and interpret incoming information in a characteristic way—a way that reflects the dominant situational or circumstantial feeling or need-states of the perceiver. Thus, a hungry man is unusually attentive to information concerning his access to food, and will tend to project "food-meaning" onto even vaguely relevant information. Similarly, I will argue in the text that the characteristic mind-set of a president is preoccupation with his personal accountability for anything of importance that happens during his administration. Accordingly, he will monitor and interpret incoming information largely in terms of its potential for reflecting favorably or unfavorably on his performance.

4. The concept of "self" may be defined as the "accumulated meaning one forges about himself as a consequence of his mediation between internal feeling states and external demands through the course of his life" (Tiedeman and O'Hara, 1963). As used here, the term is synonymous with identity. Among the important components of self-definition: (1) *competencies* (who I am is to a great extent determined by what I have shown that I can do); (2) *aspirations* (who I am now will be greatly enhanced if I am able to do what I think I can do); (3) *values* (certain things and not others are worth doing; certain ways of

behaving are appropriate and other ways are not). Of particular importance here is that people and presidents strive to live up to their self-conceptions, and that they experience considerable discomfort when competencies, aspirations, or values are threatened or disconfirmed by external events. See Wells and Marwell, *Self-Esteem*, 1976.

5. An interesting piece of research which clearly reveals the special impact of responsibility is Bourne's (1971) study of a helicopter medical aid team and a Special Forces group on hazardous duty in Viet Nam. Bourne conducted regular psychiatric interviews and gathered physiochemical data during episodes of quiet and combat. He found significant differences between officers and enlisted men on his chemical measures of stress reaction under combat conditions, with the officers registering the higher levels of adrenal secretion. The indication was that, as a result of the responsibilities and uncertainties of leadership, the officers experienced greater stress in response to the same conditions.

6. Harold Laski (1940, p. 55) writes: "The president is the subject of compulsions which begin to operate from the day he has been nominated as a candidate. . . . It is not, I think, an exaggeration to say that the day of a successful election is the day on which the president ceases to be a free man." Echoing this sentiment is Theodore Sorensen (1965, pp. 227, 229), who describes the feelings in the Kennedy camp on election day:

> He was jubilant about his victory. At the same time he was deeply touched by it. . . . Within our own borders still more pigeons were coming home to roost. The third recession in seven years had caused the highest unemployment in over twenty years. The highest deficit in the nation's international balance of payments during peacetime had depleted our gold reserves to their lowest level in over twenty years. The growing frustrations of our oppressed Negro population, the growing cost of subsidizing large farms, the growing number of overcrowded college classrooms and uncared-for elder citizens—all these and more, Kennedy knew, were not merely matters for Democratic campaign talk, but concrete problems about to confront him.

7. Examples are plentiful, but two will suffice. On January 20, 1961, Dwight D. Eisenhower (1965, p. 618) reports: "So, after the now President Kennedy had repeated the traditional, "so help me God," Mamie and I, making our way toward a side exit, made a fantastic discovery. We were free—as only private citizens in a democratic nation can be free." And on January 20, 1969, Lyndon Johnson (1971, p. 566) writes:

I heard Richard Nixon conclude his oath of office with the words "so help me God." To me, they were welcome words. I remember two thoughts running through my mind: first, that I would not have to face the decision any more of taking any step, in the Middle East or elsewhere, that might lead to world conflagration—the nightmare of my having to be the man who pressed the button to start World War III was passing; and second, that I had fervently sought peace through every available channel and at every opportunity and could have done no more.

8. Career psychologists, notably Donald Super (1963), present considerable empirical evidence in support of the notion that a person strives to implement his self-concept by choosing to enter the occupation he sees as most likely to permit him self-expression.

9. Probably the most striking example of the latter was Polk's morally questionable orchestration of the Mexican War for the thinly disguised purpose of acquiring Texas and California (See Bailey, 1966). The point is that any president sufficiently determined to have his way will be emboldened, by the liberties with the truth his symbolic and advocacy functions have already accustomed him to take, to employ such means whenever more legitimate avenues appear closed to him. See Chapter 4.

10. See Introduction, Note 13.

Crises are by no means the only source of individual stress. All of us encounter a variety of stress stimuli in our daily lives and high level policy makers probably experience more stress than most people.

HERMANN AND HERMANN, *"Maintaining the Quality of Decision-Making in Foreign Policy Crises"*

In their review of "Human Reactions to Stress," Janis and Leventhal (1968) note that there is no generally agreed-on definition of psychological stress but that for most writers the term designates a broad class of events involving interaction between *extreme environmental stimuli* and the *adjustive capacities of the organism*. Basowitz and his colleagues (1955) note that the term "stress" is frequently used to designate certain kinds of stimulating conditions without regard for response. Such stimuli are considered stressful because of their assumed or potential capacity for inducing emotional tension and for interfering with normal cognitive or judgmental processes. Although individual stress is widely considered to have three components—a stimulus, a response, and an intervening

STRESS:
The Rorschach
Test
3

psychological process (Lazarus, 1966)—it has been firmly established that people vary in their perceptions of and reactions to stress (Lacey, 1959). The same is true of presidents. But by any fair measure, certain features of the presidential role must be considered stressful.

Because he functions as mediator and crisis manager for the political system, it is assured that any president will be continuously beset by external demands that qualify as "extreme environmental stimuli" for three reasons. They are numerous, to the point of overload. They are intermittantly intense, as with crises. And they frequently conflict, forcing the president to make choices.

NUMEROUS DEMANDS

Prior to the Executive Reorganization Act of 1939, presidents were obliged to cope personally with all but the most trivial of incoming business. The experience of John Quincy Adams, recorded more than a hundred years before the passage of that Act, is not untypical of presidents up to and including FDR:

> The succession of visitors from my breakfasting to my dining is inexpressibly distressing, and now that members of Congress come and absorb my evening hours, it induces a physical impossibility that I should keep up with the stream of time in my record. An hour's walk before daylight is my only exercize for the day. Then to dress and breakfast I have scarce an hour. Then five-and-twenty visitors, or more, from ten of the morning till five in the afternoon leave me not a moment of leisure for reflection or for writing. By the time evening approaches, my strength and spirit are both exhausted (John Quincy Adams, *Diary*, December 7, 1826).

The Reorganization Act began a geometric proliferation of staff support for the president. As of February, 1977, it was reported that President Carter enjoyed the assistance of no fewer than 485 White House staff members. Obviously, assistance of this magnitude allows contemporary presidents to be more selective than the beleaguered Adams was able to be in deciding which of the endless stream of issues require personal attention. George Reedy (1973) argues that his staff resources enable a president to do as little as he wants to. And some presidents, notably Coolidge and Eisenhower, have delegated responsibilities freely, divorcing themselves almost entirely from the hectic flow of business into the White House.

But the norm that has emerged since World War II has been far more grueling, and is reminiscent of Adams's daily routine. Truman's (1956, p. 1) well-known characterization of this aspect of his experience suggests why a burgeoning staff may not relieve a modern president's feeling that he must be vigilant:

> Within the first few months I discovered that being a President is like riding a tiger. A man has to keep on riding or be swallowed. The fantastically crowded nine months of 1945 taught me that a President is either constantly on top of events, or if he hesitates, events will soon be on top of him. I never felt that I could let up for a moment.

The fact is that presidents find they must spend long hours attending to work only they can do. Kennedy and Johnson are reputed to have worked sixteen-hour days, interspersed with naps. Gerald Ford said in an interview with CBS news that he spent at least fifteen hours a day at work. And Hugh Sidey (*Time*, May 9, 1977) reports that, early in his term, Jimmy Carter was forced to expand his planned fifty-five hour work week to upward of eighty hours in order to accomodate the demands on his time posed by meetings and paperwork.

Workdays and workweeks like these are physically and emotionally draining. But the volume of demands may prove stressful for reasons other than sheer physical or psychological overload. No president can attend personally to all of the potentially important demands, no matter how many hours he devotes to his work. He is forced to delegate. But delegation does not relieve his burden. Though others may do his work for him, Watergate makes it inescapably clear that the president cannot evade responsibility for acts undertaken by others in his name. By delegating he surrenders control, but not responsibility—a major contributor to psychological stress (Bourne, 1971).

INTENSE DEMANDS

The occasional intensity of a president's problems arises from his responsibility for crisis management. A crisis can be defined as any international or domestic situation that poses a major threat to one or more goals or other values important to the United States (Hermann and Hermann, 1975). Distinguishing characteristics of crises include *surprise*—they frequently emerge suddenly and without warning—and *time limits*: Decisions must be made without adequate time either for the collection of relevant information or for the careful and dispassionate review of options. Crises thus severely hamper the prospects for rational decision-making (George 1975).

Psychological stress is experienced when the president interprets the threat to the nation's goals as also endangering something of high value to himself as an individual (Hermann and Hermann, 1975). Since he is personally responsible for the welfare of the nation in any emergency situation, we can assume that any president will feel personally involved in any significant crisis, and thus is likely to experience such classic stress reactions as emotional arousal, distress, fear, or anxiety.

Crises are highly unpredictable and have been visited unevenly upon the presidents. Alfred de Grazia (1969) has scorned the crisis management image of the presidency as largely mythological, arguing that presidents often manipulate or create crises to suit their own purposes. The ratio of cosmetic to genuine crises would probably support de Grazia's point. But the fact remains that there are intermittent crises, demanding swift presidential action, whose consequences will seem vague and frightening at the moment of decision. Equally important is that the prospect of unanticipated crisis always exists around the presidency, and may produce a stress reaction that Janis and Leventhal (1968) term "indiscriminate vigilance," an anxious wariness that can border on paranoia. Just such a mind-set pervaded the presidency during the Cold War era, and again later as an obviously anxious and fearful Richard Nixon sought to forestall a variety of imagined threats to the presidency by surreptitious means. As the Nixon case illustrates, a president need only perceive that he faces an emergency in order to experience a stress reaction. Given that the office is the locus for national crisis management, the climate engendered by the reality, perception, or anticipation of grave trouble will inevitably give rise to psychological stress for the president.

CONFLICTING DEMANDS

As mediator, the president is the lightning rod for the political system. An important source of the dilemmas which are his daily bread is his responsibility for reconciling the conflicting desires of major social, economic, and political interests (Neustadt, 1969). Conflicting demands translate into irreconcilable expectations for presidential support or action. The president is repeatedly enjoined to find some middle ground between labor and management, oil companies and environmentalists, hawks and doves, young and old, rich and poor, white and black, liberals and conservatives, and between innumerable other polarities that constantly arise from the diversity of values and interests that co-exist in this society. Issues significant enough to reach his desk routinely embody multiple, conflicting, and competing values. It is rarely possible to formulate a single yardstick for decision that will aggregate and satisfy all of the contending interests. Thus, it is a complex and difficult matter to judge what course of action is best in any given situation. The president repeatedly faces painful trade-off problems of this nature. And such circumstances can be extremely stressful for the decision-maker (George, 1975).

Illustrations of presidential discomfort in the face of such value conflicts are numerous, and run the gamut of character types.[1] Passive-positive Warren G. Harding (quoted in Fenno, 1959, p. 36), for example, facing a controversial decision on tax policy, complained to a friend:

John, I can't make a damn thing out of this tax problem. I listen to one side and they seem right, and then God! I talk to the other side and they seem just as right, and there I am where I started. I know somewhere there is a book that would give me the truth, but hell, I couldn't read the book. I know somewhere there is an economist who knows the truth, but I don't know where to find him and haven't the sense to know him and trust him when I did find him.

And active-positive John Kennedy, piqued at the reaction of the business community to his attempts at wage–price mediation, exclaimed bitterly to Arthur Schlesinger (1965, p. 641):

I understand better every day why Roosevelt, who started out such a mild fellow, ended up so ferociously anti-business. It is hard as hell to be friendly with people who keep trying to cut your legs off. . . . There are about ten thousand people in the country involved in this—bankers, industrialists, lawyers, publishers, politicians—a small group, but doing everything they can to say we are going into a depression because business has no confidence in the administration. They are starting to call me the Democratic Hoover. Well, we're not going to take that.

Even so exuberant a warrior as Franklin D. Roosevelt (quoted in Blum, 1972, 447–48), a man who fomented and appeared to thrive on controversy, nonetheless found it straining when called upon to mediate personally between embattled factions inside his official family:

Angered as always when his subordinates fought in his presence, Roosevelt pounded the table. "I am the boss," he said again. "I am the one who gets the rap if we get licked in Congress, and I am the one who is in control. You people [Morgenthau and Byrnes] have to get together on a tax bill and then we can work for the Treasury to present it. . .and the other people to work behind the scenes."

And the first active-positive president, Thomas Jefferson (quoted in Malone, 1970, p. 85), found that mediating among the demands of his supporters for political appointments was vexing in the extreme:

Toward the end of his presidency, addressing a friendly state governor, Jefferson reflected that solicitations for office were the most painful incidents to which an executive magistrate was exposed, and that the "gift of office" was his most dreadful burden. "A [president] who wishes to make it an engine of self-elevation, may do wonders with it," he said; "but to one who wishes to use it conscientiously for the public good without regard to the ties of blood and friendship, it creates enmities without numbers, many open, but more secret, and saps the happiness and peace of his life."

These examples illustrate emotional reactions before, during, and after decisions aimed at resolving significant value conflicts.[2] They help to make the point that stress reactions to forced-choice situations (in these cases uncertainty, confusion, vindictiveness, fear, anger, and anguish), are not restricted to ill-suited character types.

Stress is increased by intense public interest in how the president acts to resolve contending values. This serves to fix his responsibility for the outcome firmly in the public's eyes.[3] Though such trade-offs come to him willy-nilly, and do not necessarily involve issues on which he has chosen to stake his prestige, the glare of publicity insures that he will have considerable personal and professional stake in the outcome.

In many respects, these are no-win situations. Any action that he takes is bound to give offense to someone. Yet his political viability is contingent upon maintaining an "intricately interwoven and unstable collection of feelings and attitudes held by those whose cooperation and goodwill are essential to his effectiveness" (Neustadt, 1960). The Washington community is central, but hinges its approbation on its reading of the president's standing with the general public as well as with various specialized publics. The perversity of this situation from the president's point of view is illustrated by Mueller's (1973) "coalition of minorities effect," which shows that it is much easier to alienate segments of the Washington community than to win or keep friends by actions designed to have broad appeal.[4]

Add to this the fact that any president, almost regardless of what he does or says about anything, falls under consistent and widely publicized critical attack while he is in office. The honeymoon period and the aftermaths of dramatic successes are exceptions. But a seemingly automatic decline in presidential popularity with increasing tenure has been fully documented (Mueller, 1973; Roper, 1968). The institutionalized negativity of press coverage is known to have disturbed and irritated nearly every president (Coyle, 1960). Presidents must contend with unrelenting negative feedback. Despite public demurrals, they find it painful and vexing.

Thus we see that stressful exposures of varying kinds and intensities are imbedded in the routine experience of any president. Numerous demands are his daily fare. Conflict situations are only slightly less frequent. And crises, though episodic and unpredictable, stand as latent threats to presidential tranquility. Some sense of the feeling states occasioned by these exposures was captured in the presidential expressions quoted above.[5] Now is the time to look more closely at those feeling states, and at the kind of behavior likely to be associated with them.

PSYCHOLOGICAL MEANING OF PRESIDENTIAL STRESS

I noted at the outset of this chapter that psychologists define stress as any stimulation extreme enough to induce emotional tension or interfere with normal cognitive or judgmental processes. In Chapter 2, I mentioned that certain kinds of stress—specifically stress which is mild in intensity and short in duration—can have generally beneficial consequences. Good stress serves to mobilize the individual's physical and psychological resources, increase his motivation, and discipline his efforts, and, when he is able to resolve the stressful circumstances to his own satisfaction, such stress fills him with a sense of competence and efficacy (Costello and Zalkind, 1963).

In characterizing the president's role demands as numerous, intense, and conflicting, I have argued that the president's exposure to stress is chronic and intense. It is not likely to be perceived as challenging and invigorating because it is too pervasive, too unrelieved, and, for the most part, too independent of presidential control.

But if we can agree that presidents are exposed mostly to bad stress, likely to be perceived as burdensome, it is still not clear why chronic, intense stress is unpleasant. What makes presidential stress burdensome? What is it that gives extreme stimulation the power to disrupt psychological functioning? Why does stress induce emotional tension? The answer is that it threatens something near and dear to any president: the status and security of his identity. The authorities cited (Hermann and Hermann, 1975; George, 1975) and the illustrations given earlier suggest that exposures are stressful when they threaten to undermine or to call into question the president's competencies, his public standing, his political power, his personal and political values, or his resolve—all important components of his self-concept. It is in this light that feeling states like fear, anguish, confusion, disorientation, anger, or emotional arousal begin to make sense. These are not the kinds of feelings expressed by those who are disinterested or detached. They are the emotions of those who are personally and irrevocably engaged—by difficult circumstances that do not admit of flight or easy avoidance. Thus, it is useful to conceive of the touchpoint of stress as the self-concept. The psychological meaning of presidential stress can be grasped only if its status as *self-relevant* stimulation is recognized. It is the fact of personal responsibility that engages the self-concept, and the possibility of failure that threatens it (Lewin, 1936).

PSYCHOLOGICAL AND BEHAVIORAL
CONSEQUENCES OF CHRONIC STRESS

Table 1 schematizes the patterns of presidential stress from its origin in role demands through its impact on the president's orientations and behavior, which remain to be discussed. It is worth noting again that the focus is upon long-term adaptations rather than upon situational responses. Also worth repeating is my acknowledgment that

Table 1   Patterns of Presidential Stress

ROLE DEMAND	INEVITABLE EXPOSURE	PSYCHOLOGICAL MEANING
Mediator	Conflict, Controversy	Personal Responsibility
Crisis Manager	Grave Uncertainty	Threat to Self-Concept

PSYCHOLOGICAL EXPERIENCE	CUMULATIVE PSYCHOLOGICAL IMPACT[a]	PRESIDENTIAL BEHAVIOR[a]
Chronic, Intense Stress	Indiscriminant Vigilance	Decline in Performance Effectiveness
	Excessive Energy Consumption	Physical Deterioration
	Emotional Instability	Psychological Disorientation
		'Formalistic' Management System

[a] Varies with individual differences,

individuals will vary in their psychological and behavioral adaptations to this and to each of the other pressures of the presidency.[6] However, stress is an important *standardizing* force, capable of shaping and channeling both attitudes and behavior along characteristic lines for people in general and for presidents in general.

The research literature agrees on three psycho-physical responses to chronic, intense stress. The first, indiscriminate vigilance, was mentioned earlier in connection with crises. But such a mind-set is encouraged by the general unpredictability and uncertainty surrounding the multiple and conflicting demands visited upon the White House as well. Harry Truman's "riding the tiger" comment epitomizes this mind-set. It is reasonable to expect that adjusting to his responsibilities will result not only in episodically intense mobilization of physical emotional resources, but also in a significant increase in the president's chronic level of physical and psychological mobilization as well. Lazarus (1966) reports that chronic stress produces significant chemical and autonomic physiological changes. At the very least, we can assume that the demands of the presidency, as contrasted with pre-presidential levels, will significantly increase the rate at which physical and psychological energies are consumed.

If stress continues too long, or becomes too severe for a given individual, bodily defenses eventually break down and exhaustion is experienced (Torrance, 1963; Coleman, 1960). The syndrome of excessive energy consumption is frequently accompanied by psychological disorientation, such as that allegedly experienced by Richard Nixon near the end of his Watergate ordeal (Woodward and Bernstein, 1976), or by emotional or nervous breakdowns, such as that of Woodrow Wilson following upon his defeat in the League of Nations dispute (George and George, 1956). More common is a marked physical deterioration: heart trouble, ulcers, or other diseases of adaptation (Coleman, 1960). The health records of the presidents circumstantially corroborate the assumed presence of chronic, intense stress. Milton Plesur (1974, p. 189) concludes that the average duration of presidential life has been shorter than might have been expected.

PERFORMANCE EFFECTIVENESS: THE "FORMALISTIC" MANAGEMENT SYSTEM

The most tangible evidence of a president's personal reaction to stress is the organizational system he establishes to process the demands of office. Since few features of the White House command structure remain unchanged across presidencies, the system a president imposes can be equated with his response to a Rorschach test: It is extraordinarily revealing of his nature, his sensitivities, and his vulnerabilities.

From the standpoint of his effective performance of presidential functions, and from the standpoint of such democratic values as openness and accessibility, the least desirable management structure a president can impose is what Richard Tanner Johnson (1974) has termed a "formalistic" system. Unfortunately, it is also the system that provides the greatest amount of protection against stressful exposures and the greatest amount of presidential control over the flow of his work. Both of these points can be made by examining the nature of the formalistic system. How does such a system cope with the numerous, intense, and conflicting demands of the presidency?

The formalistic system corresponds closely to a classic bureaucracy. It embodies a hierarchy of authority, functional specialization, communication channels, and clearly specified procedures. It stands in sharp contrast to collegial or competitive organizations, which de-emphasize authority relationships and encourage conflict as a means of stimulating creativity (Johnson, 1974).

The formal system isolates the top man by situating him at the apex of the pyramid amidst strict controls which regulate the access of people and the flow of information to him. Demands enter the system at the bottom, where they are allocated among functional specialists for disposition. Conflicting demands are sorted into alternatives with clearly specified advantages and disadvantages before they are sent up the hierarchy for decision, which usually takes place below the top level. The president sees only those issues which have been flagged for his attention. He works alone or in the company of a few select aides. His environment is controlled, stressing orderliness and tranquility, and minimizing the pressures of time when possible.

On its face, this system appears to have merit. It is rational and orderly, and distributes burdens realistically. The problem, of course, is that it imposes an artificial stability on what is essentially an unstable set of circumstances. Effective performance of the presidential functions demands unusual flexibility and acute sensitivity to subtle changes in the political climate. A formal management system reduces stress by routinizing the work flow, displacing much of it away from the president, and increasing the opportunities for presidential privacy and tranquility. But it simultaneously threatens to filter and distort information as it travels up the hierarchy, to sanitize and defuse the passions surrounding issues, and thus to misrepresent their political meaning and significance. And it is likely to reduce the speed with which the president and his machinery are able to respond to emergency situations (Johnson, 1974). The system thus places highly undesirable constraints on the president's ability to discharge his responsibilities.

The argument that his management system reveals the president—to the public and even to himself—is well illustrated by the case of Richard Nixon. Nixon began his presidency with plans that would prove to be inconsistent with his innate vulnerabilities and predilections. He contemplated an open administration, characterized by the vigorous clash of ideas and by FDR-like access to himself for warring advisors, and he cherished an idealized image of himself as a benevolent, Eisenhower-like figure, dispassionately resolving disputes in the interests of good policy (Rather and Gates, 1974). It soon became apparent that he was temperamentally unsuited to the role of conflict mediator. He gradually excised his most colorful and disputatious advisors (Moynihan, Connally) and insulated himself behind such men as the sober-sided gatekeeper Haldeman, men who could shield him from the unpleasant need to deal with interpersonal conflict.

Nixon, of course, is widely viewed as one of the least suitable personalities ever to occupy the presidency. The only other modern president to employ a formal system, Dwight D. Eisenhower, has received mixed reviews. But the differences between these men does make it clear that reliance on a formal system as a means of coping with stress is not limited to pathological characters. [7] It is quite conceivable that an active-positive president, confronting an especially turbulent power situation or climate of expectations, might fall back on such an arrangement out of self-defense. Moreover, Eisenhower's heart trouble and Nixon's Watergate difficulties show how events can pierce even the most impenetrable of organizational barriers to disturb the tranquility of the president.

CONCLUSION

The paradox is clear. Any president is routinely beset by stresses capable of undermining the physical and mental health even of "wise and prudent athletes."[8] Presidents willing to expose themselves to the full force of this pressure retain the flexibility and access to information necessary to function effectively, but they risk significant loss of physical and mental vitality in the process. Those who elect the pattern of self-protective adjustment just described buy an ephemeral tranquility that reduces the quality of their performance by increasing the likelihood of misjudgment, misinterpretation, and unresponsiveness. Over the long run it is evident that stress may be increased as the consequences of ill-conceived or misinformed decisions manifest themselves, as we have seen in the cases of Nixon and Eisenhower.

A question that will arise repeatedly in these chapters describing the pressures of the presidency is: What can be done? How can the stress inevitably attending the central executive function be reduced to a human scale? It is idle to expect any natural lessening of the burdens described in this chapter. There will, of course, be periodic lulls and occasionally uneventful presidencies, but our national experience suggests that these are few and far between.

We are left, then, with the choice of continuing our present course, hoping against hope that the electoral process can produce an individual with personal resources sufficient to carry him through his term, if not through a normal lifespan *or* of considering structural and procedural changes that might make the job consistent with human limitations. The fact is that psychological stress threatens both the well-being of the president *and* the effectiveness with which he performs his functions. Reform can address either problem, but its ultimate purpose must be to protect the effectiveness of the presidency rather than to increase the personal comfort of presidents. Of course the issues are related. A president strained beyond his capacity to endure cannot be as effective as one who feels secure and equal to the demands.

One obvious remedy would be to remove some of the responsibilities of the presidency, transferring them to other governmental bodies. For example, Stephen Hess (1976) has argued that it is inappropriate to expect presidents to manage the bureaucracy, and that policy implementation and follow-up should be the work of Cabinet officers and the Departments. This has an alluring quality to it—similar in appeal to the cry of the 1937 Brownlow Commission that "the President needs help," which precipitated the tremendous growth in the White House staff. But the limits should also be apparent. Among these are sharp restrictions on the number of specific duties and responsibilities that can be relocated without stripping the presidency of its historical identity. But the devolution of some functions is appropriate and could reduce the number—if not the conflicts and intensities—of the demands presidents confront. For example, Hess's argument that the imbalance in size between the White House staff and the federal bureaucracy makes it impossible for the president to effectively monitor the output side of bureaucratic performance is quite plausible, and could justify a relocation of this responsibility. But we must bear in mind that it is the responsibility—not simply the sheer physical workload—that is the major cause of stress. Thus, reducing the workload—like increasing the president's staff support—is a partial solution at best. We are obliged to look further.

There are certain measures a president can take in his own behalf. He might employ the self-help and stress-reduction techniques currently in vogue in the society at large. Meditation, self-hypnosis, mind control, and other self-administered nostrums aimed at the cultivation of psychological detachment from life's trials and tribulations are as available to presidents as they are to the rest of us. And there is some evidence that these can work for individuals who take them seriously. In a similar vein, the deliberate cultivation of certain values or philosophical stances—such as a "Madisonian" view of the presidency,[9] a deterministic view of the universe, or a religious faith in a benevolent deity—could reduce a president's feelings of personal vulnerability. Indeed, if the truth were known, religious faith would likely be revealed as the major private coping resource used by presidents. Yet concerned citizens and scholars cannot invest much hope in these methods, for their efficacy will not be uniform across presidents, and they are beyond our power to legislate. Their use and effectiveness depends strictly on the private values of individual presidents—something they rarely share with us and something that changes with each change of administrations. Such remedies thus stand outside the public domain.

Another less private reform a president could institute in his own behalf might increase the prospects for quality decisions under stress, but would do little to reduce his personal pain and suffering. I refer here to the decision-making procedures a president employs in working toward his important judgments. Clearly the stressful milieu described in this chapter stands as a threat to rational decision-making. Given this fact, a president can move to protect the quality of his decisions by establishing thorough and carefully designed procedures which must be exhausted before important decisions are reached. The distorting effects of fear, anxiety, and uncertainty could be minimized if procedures like those described by Janis and Mann (1977) or George (1975) were scrupulously observed. Such procedures place emphasis on compensating for emotional distortions by thoroughly canvassing broad ranges of alternatives, by careful collection and review of information, by specification of the tradeoffs associated with each alternative, and by the inclusion of fresh, unbiased perspectives in the deliberations—all aimed at forcing the decision-maker to open himself to reality.

But failing a legal requirement that such procedures be used, their use would depend on the situational discretion of presidents, which itself is influenced by their emotional responses to issues and events. A president may resolve to follow such a program in a tranquil moment, only to abandon it under the press of emergency circumstances. The point is that the president's personal state requires attention in devising reforms. Rational procedures are obviously necessary, but just as obviously they are not sufficient unto themselves. Reform proposals must somehow grapple with the question of how the president can—in the face of his turbulent and pressing responsibilities—maintain an objective and balanced personal state.

Mention can finally be made of a structural reform which addresses the president's personal state and is consistent with the use of rational procedures, but which is politically unrealistic. That reform is a collegial, or plural presidency. Such a reform could encourage the use of rational decision-making procedures while simultaneously reducing the psychological burden on the solitary president. By creating a group of co-equal presidents, we could give rise to circumstances which reduced the impact of stress. The reason is, as Schacter (1959) and other psychologists have shown, that precisely the same stresses—when shared by others—produce far fewer stress reactions than when borne alone. People in groups draw strength from each other and do a better job of living with stress than do lone individuals.

Though potentially the most effective remedy, this is also the least likely to be adopted. It would require massive change—always difficult to produce in this political system. It is justly suspected of raising as many problems as it solves. And it would fundamentally alter an institution which is at the core of our national identity.

We are left, then, with a collection of flawed possibilities. Each lacks some critical element necessary to a solution. I review the options more thoroughly in the concluding chapter. For now, it is clear that no quick and easy remedies to the problems posed by stress are available. If structural and procedural reform is impossible or imperfect, our dependence on the character, competencies, and endurance capacities of those we elect would appear to be increased. Whether character can bear the added responsibility is considered in Chapter 7.

Stress alone would be sufficient cause to look closely at the prospects for reform, and at what we can expect from character. But stress is not alone. The other vectors of influence are somewhat less debilitating for the president. But they are no less threatening to the adequacy of his performance. Even deference, the most beguiling and flattering of presidential exposures, poses important obstacles to presidential effectiveness.

NOTES

1. The references to character types made in this and subsequent chapters are to Barber's (1977) four-fold classification of the presidents. Barber's scheme is analyzed in some detail in Chapter 7, but capsule

summaries of his types will be useful here. *Active-Positive*: high energy level, enjoyment of activity. Success in relating to the environment. Orientation toward productiveness as a value. Flexible and rational style. The *only one* of Barber's four types to which he attributed high self-esteem. In Barber's judgment, this type is best equipped to handle the demands of the presidency (FDR, Truman, Kennedy, Ford, and Carter are examples). *Active-Negative*: contradiction between intense effort and low emotional reward for that effort. Low self esteem. Tendency to rigidity under certain kinds of pressure, and to persist in failing courses of action (Wilson, Hoover, LBJ, and Nixon are examples). *Passive-Positive*: receptive, compliant, other-directed character who seeks affection in return for being agreeable. Contradiction between low self-esteem and a superficial optimism. Danger of drift under a passive-positive president (Taft and Harding are examples). *Passive-Negative*: does little and enjoys it less. Orientation toward doing dutiful service as compensation for low self-esteem based on a sense of uselessness. Lacks the experience and flexibility to perform effectively as a political leader. Tendency to withdraw and avoid conflict by emphasizing vague principles and procedural arrangements. Emphasis on civic virtue (Coolidge and Eisenhower are examples). Though I will adduce evidence (see Chapter 7) to support Barber's implicit contention that the high self-esteem character is the best equipped to handle the presidency, the point I am trying to make in these chapters on the pressures is that character offers no secure solution to the problem of withstanding such pressure. As the quotes reprinted in the text show, Active-Positives are by no means immune to the negative influences of the presidential experience (see Preface, footnote 14).

2. Presidents, of course, rarely lose sleep deciding against the interests of non-supporters. Strain and discomfort arise when, for one reason or another, the president finds himself committed to a course of action he knows may alienate loyal supporters and perhaps convert them into political adversaries (McFarland, 1969). The experience of Chester A. Arthur in connection with Civil Service Reform is a case in point. Himself a promoter and product of the spoils system as Collector of the Port of New York, Arthur attained the vice-presidential nomination as a consequence of his loyal subservience to the political machine headed by Senator Conkling of New York. When he assumed the presidency upon Garfield's death, it was widely expected that he would

remain loyal to the Conkling machine. Instead, he outraged his former allies by, among other things, supporting and winning passage of the Pendleton Act. He enjoyed wide public support for this effort, but so estranged himself from his own party that not only was he unable to win the party's nomination for president in 1884, he even failed to receive a nomination from New York Republicans for a seat in the U.S. Senate. His failure to rally the party behind his reform efforts cost him the presidency, and the strain of the conflict apparently hastened his death, which occurred some twenty months after he left the White House.

3. Fred Greenstein (1974, p. 146) observes:

> In the case of the central, energizing institution in the modern American political system, the Presidency, the very strength that accrues to the President by his singular visibility and his capacity to become the receptacle of widespread personal hopes and aspirations carries with it. . .an obvious weakness: if things go wrong, who else is there to blame? The depression becomes "Hoover's depression"; the "mess in Washington" becomes Truman's or Nixon's, even before a proper assessment of responsibility has taken place.

4. See note 2 above for an illustration of Mueller's coalition of minorities effect.

5. Additional expressions of presidential pain are cited in Finer (1960, pp. 36–37). Some representative quotes: "Grant declared that he was weary of office: 'I never wanted to get out of a place as much as I did to get out of the Presidency.' Hayes wrote in his diary in 1879 that Mrs. Hayes agreed with him in saying, 'Well, I am heartily tired of this life of bondage, responsibility, and toil. I wish it was at an end.' After four years in the White House, Cleveland wrote: 'You cannot imagine the relief which has come to me with the termination of my official term.' Finally, in our own time, President Wilson found that he had to breakfast at five or six and work well into the night to fulfill the responsibilities of the office as he felt them, commenting also that the burden would kill him."

6. One intriguing "coping mechanism" characterizes many of the presidents who fit into Barber's passive-positive and passive-negative categories: the tendency to identify with Madisonian, or strict-constructionist models of the presidency. This is "coping" in that identification with such a model serves to limit and clarify those issues for which a president is obliged to feel responsible. Since Madisonian presidents are free to disclaim any responsibilities not expressly en-

joined by the Constitution, they can enjoy freedom from psychological guilt should they decide to ignore demands made upon them by those who entertain Hamiltonian or Jeffersonian conceptions of executive responsibility. Thus, Eisenhower seemed blithely indifferent to the dissatisfaction with his "caretaker" presidency expressed by the liberal community. In the parlance of social psychology, the "sent" role differs sharply from the "received" role (Katz and Kahn, 1966). For a similar distinction between externally given demands and an individual's conception of his role responsibilities, see Levinson, 1971. For a clarification of strict-constructionist interpretations of the presidency, see Stokes (1976), "Whig Conceptions of Executive Power," *Presidential Studies Quarterly*, 6:16–35. For further discussion of this and other individual differences between presidents, see Chapter 7.

7. Preference for a formalistic management system is consistent with the kinds of psychological defenses (avoidance, withdrawal) associated in the research literature either with very high self-esteem (Wells and Marwell, 1976), or with very low self-esteem (Sniderman, 1975). Open and flexible defenses, on the other hand, have been shown in some research to characterize those with medium levels of self-esteem (Cole et. al., 1967). Setting this against Barber's categories, we can expect not only that selection of this management style would not be limited to active-negatives, but also that it would not always be avoided by active-positives, the only one of his types to which he attributes high self-esteem.

8. Woodrow Wilson's characterization of the "small class" of people able to bear up under the cognitive and physical demands of the presidency.

9. See Note 6 above.

The effect of power and publicity on all men is the aggravation of self, a sort of tumor that ends by killing the victim's sympathies; a diseased appetite, like a passion for drink and perverted tastes; one can scarcely use expressions too strong to describe the violence of egotism it stimulates.

The Education of Henry Adams

The fear of separating the leaders from the led has informed the design of governments since the Golden Age of Greece. In the United States, this fear helped win support for the decision to create separate institutions that would share power. But the abiding need of citizens for a human symbol of government, for a personalized source of reassurance, inspiration, and a sense of legitimacy, led to an investment—in the presidency and the president—of an aura of majesty, splendor, and magnificence fully equal to the most resplendent European monarchies of the eighteenth century.

If, as Lord Acton warned, power corrupts, one of the reasons is the way we treat the powerful. Consider what it means to be elected and to serve as president of the United States. First and most important, the presidency is the premier station in all of American life. To

DEFERENCE: The Impact Of Status Inequality

4

win the presidency is to experience the ultimate in self-validating achievement. As Harold Laski (1940, p. 33) observes: "In general, it is almost true to say that entrance upon the office itself breeds self-confidence." There is no higher ambition, and no greater personal prize to be had in this or any other society. Added to this massive personal vindication is the fact of personal control over tremendous institutional power. The president was chosen from numerous competitors to decide when and whether to use the considerable might of the republic, in all its various forms.

Third is the experience of abrupt transition from a lowly to an exalted status. The president began as a commoner. In the United States, one cannot be born to such a station. Although we have had a number of patrician presidents, most presidents come from modest, middle-class backgrounds. And even the advantages of wealth and family station cannot equip a person for the heady treatment that is reserved for the president.

These things argue that his elevation to the presidency will have some impact on any president; but what are the consequences of being the human symbol of the majesty of the United States Government? There are two popular schools of thought. One is reflected in the disgust and the fear expressed by Henry Adams and Lord Acton: Such a station cannot help but aggravate a violent egomania, a swelling of the head. This view is bolstered by the long-familiar hypothesis that power seekers aspire to high office as a compensation for deep-seated feelings of inferiority and inadequacy (Lasswell, 1951). It is realistic to expect, from one who has hungered and struggled to prove himself, that he will revel in the glories of power, once attained. And it is also realistic to expect that he will keep striving to quell his private fears with more and more evidence of his power and potency.

The second view, part of the mythology of the presidency, is that great power and great status enables he who wields it. Common, even mean-spirited men, once elected, rise above baser motives and beyond their own limits to the altruistic and judicious use of power. And indeed there have been presidents—notably Chester A. Arthur and Martin Van Buren—whose behavior supports this view. Based on their analysis of these and other presidents, Rogow and Lasswell (1963) conclude that, to some extent, the prestige and stature of the presidency have insulated it from becoming a setting for corruption.

In the wake of Watergate and Viet Nam, it has become apparent that such a sanguine view of the presidency is misplaced. More recent analyses of the presidency conclude that the deification of presidents usually has undesirable consequences, both for the president and for the political system. For example, George Reedy (1970, p. 10) writes:

> The environment of deference, approaching sycophancy, helps to foster another insidious factor. It is a belief that the president and a few of his most trusted advisors are possessed of a special knowledge which must be closely held within a small group lest the plans and the designs of the United States be anticipated and frustrated by enemies.

And Thomas Cronin (1975, p. 33), despoiler of the myth of the "textbook" presidency, argues:

> The significance of the textbook presidency is that the whole is greater than the sum of the parts. It presents a cumulative presidential image, a legacy of past glories and impressive performances—the exalted dignity of Lincoln, the Wilsonian eloquence, the robust vitality of the Roosevelts, the benign smile and lasting popularity of Eisenhower, the inspirational spirit of Kennedy, the legislative wizardry of Lyndon Johnson, the globetrotting of the first-term Nixon—which endows the White House with singular mystique and almost magical qualities. According to this image, the office of the presidency seems to clothe its occupants in strength and dignity, in might and right, and only men of the caliber of Lincoln, the Roosevelts, or Wilson can seize the chalice of opportunity, create the vision, and rally the American public around that vision. Collectively, this portrait of the presidency can hardly help but stretch the student imagination; literally, it boggles the mind.

Thus, the exaggerated awe that has surrounded the symbolic presidency has fallen under sustained critical attack, largely because it cuts the president off from reality, and because it creates wildly unrealistic expectations in the minds of citizens. I share both of these views. But I want to concentrate, in this chapter as in the others, on the president's point of view. What can recurring exposure to deference be expected to do to the president as a person?

THE EXPOSURE: STATUS INEQUALITY

A symbol is a material object representing something immaterial.[1] As the dominant symbol of government, the president represents the values, majesty, integrity, and potency of the political system. The president is literally a walking emblem. By virtue of his position, those who encounter him face-to-face tend to invest his person with primordial, atavistic meaning. He sits in Lincoln's chair, and he speaks with the moral authority of Washington, Jefferson, Jackson, and Roosevelt. People attribute something of the luster, virtue, and competence of these giants to any president. He absorbs their colors, and this cannot help but have a significant impact on how other people relate to him.

Any president is treated with exaggerated respect, even awe, by almost anyone he encounters. From a psychological standpoint, this has one critically important consequence for him. Throughout his term of office, he can never be among equals. As long as he is in the White House, he is denied access to true peers (Reedy, 1970). Thus, the recurring exposure that emerges from his symbolic role is *status inequality*.

PSYCHOLOGICAL MEANING: DISTORTED SOCIAL COMPARISON PROCESSES

Much of the deference a president encounters is ceremonial—such as the playing of "Hail to the Chief" upon his entrance, the custom of addressing him as "Mr. President," and the practice of having him precede others through doorways. Informally, and much more significantly, deference finds expression in the near-automatic assumption that the president is uniquely gifted, specially wise, and worthy of unusual respect and attention in any interpersonal situation he confronts. As George Reedy puts it, there is no one to tell the president to go "soak his head."

To appreciate the significance of such treatment, we must begin with an understanding of how people use each other in order to stay in touch with reality. Reality-attuning information may pertain either to some external issue or event or to the self. In either case, people compare their views, ideas, and interpretations with those of others as a means of testing and refining the accuracy of their perceptions, impressions, and emotional reactions (Festinger, 1954; Radloff, 1968). Social comparison processes are the major means of reality testing and adjustment for anyone.

Simultaneously, there is an innate human tendency toward self-protection and self-enhancement. Most personality theorists agree that healthy psychological functioning requires a positive sense of self (Hall and Lindzey, 1970; Wylie, 1968; McCandless, 1961). Research has shown that people will perceive selectively in order to protect and maintain favorable self-conceptions (Katz, 1963). Unsurprisingly, there is a concomitant tendency for people in general to seek out and affiliate with those who have attitudes and values similar to their own (Aronson, 1972). Comfort, security, and self-confirmation are enhanced by association with like-minded peers.

Thus, some natural distortion in the accuracy of the interpretations that anybody's social comparison behavior can produce is implied by the innate tendency toward self-protection and enhancement. As human beings, presidents can be assumed to have the same tendency. But its consequences for their perceptions of self and of external events are likely to be magnified considerably by the status factor.

Status inequality can be expected to intensify the supportiveness with which his comparison group treats the high status figure. It is therefore likely to exaggerate the natural distortions in the accuracy with which the high status figure perceives himself and externalities. Because he is continuously exposed to artificially positive feedback, and because he, like any other person, cannot achieve total indepen- dence from the judgments of others, the president is caught in an insidious trap which obstructs his access to reality.

CUMULATIVE PSYCHOLOGICAL IMPACTS

The long-run consequences of this dynamic can be considered in two categories. The first involves perceptions of external events, and has been convincingly described by Irving Janis in his book, *Victims of Groupthink* (1972). Most presidents rely on a small group of trusted advisors to help them reach important policy decisions. In rare instances (perhaps best illustrated by Lyndon Johnson's treat- ment of his closest aides), the effects of status inequality between the president and his people may be blatant and obvious—with the president overtly using his status to bludgeon the group into rubber- stamping his preformed decisions.[2] The more likely and incalcula- bly more dangerous possibility is described by Janis (1972, p. 3):

> During the group's deliberations, the leader does *not* deliberately try to get the group to tell him what he wants to hear but is *quite sincere* in asking for honest opinions. The group members are not trans- formed into sycophants. They are not afraid to speak their minds. Nevertheless, subtle constraints, which the *leader may reinforce in- advertently*, prevent a member from fully exercising his critical powers and from openly expressing doubts when most others in the group appear to have reached a consensus [emphases mine].

Thus, neither the president nor the group may be consciously aware of the impact of the president's status, but it may still act as a si- lently decisive factor in inhibiting debate and encouraging consen- sus, to the detriment not only of an objective appraisal of specific alternatives but also of the president's long-run access to reality- attuning discussion. The consequences for the "operational codes" he develops (e.g., the accuracy of his interpretations) are obvious (George, 1969).

The second consequence concerns the effects of status inequality on perceptions of the self. Like other people, presidents will tend in the long run to be more responsive to supportive than to critical evaluations (Schacter, 1959). Furthermore, the impact of deference on the president's self-conception may well be *enhanced* by its stark contrast with the reflexive negativity of the evaluations offered by the media and other "out-group" professionals. For deference confronts the president with equally reflexive and unrealistic positive feedback. As noted in Chapter 2, his status is a ubiquitous reminder that the president has attained a position in life that is estimable in its own right, independently of the ups and downs of his daily experience. It might thus be expected to capture his attention, and even to turn his head, if only because it is a small but dependable source of personal confirmation in a milieu that repeatedly threatens to disconfirm his pretentions.

Given the role of reality-based feedback in maintaining an objective sense of self, and given the extreme and decidedly unrealistic feedback that is his daily fare, any president faces a challenge of serious proportions. He is of course aware that most judgments of him and his performance lack balance and authenticity. Yet, as a human being, he cannot achieve total independence from external judgments.

Insecure presidents may unwittingly telegraph their desire for emotional support, thus inviting and inadvertently reinforcing deferential treatment beyond the merely ceremonial.[3] For such a president, this can mean consistent exposure to inflated estimates of his prowess, his stature, and his potential influence on the course of events, all from sources he is accustomed to trusting. Woodrow Wilson's relationship with Colonel House is instructive on this point. As Alexander and Juliette George (1956, p. 124–25) observe:

> From the first, House kept assuring Wilson that he was one of the greatest men in all history. His letters were punctuated with praise: "My great and good friend"; "I think you never did anything better"; "you are so much more efficient than any public man with whom I have heretofore been in touch, that the others seem mere tyros"; "No man ever deserved better of his country"; "Your letter

of acceptance. . . is altogether the best paper of the kind that has been issued within my memory. . . ."

Furthermore:

> It would be a mistake to dismiss House as an insincere flatterer, as some historians have done. It would be more accurate, perhaps, to evaluate him as an exceedingly keen judge of what types of behavior on his part were required to keep him in good standing with Wilson. Very early in the relationship, House became aware of Wilson's extraordinary need for, and responsiveness to, praise, approval and personal devotion. He proceeded to cater to it.

> "I do not think you can ever know, my great and good friend," he wrote Wilson on May 20, 1913, "how much I appreciate your kindness to me. All that I have tried to do seems so little when measured by the returns you have made. . . . I shall believe that you will be successful in all your undertakings for, surely, no one is so well equipped as you to do what you have planned. My faith in you is as great as my love for you—more than that I cannot say."

Thus, it is apparent that his lack of access to social and interpersonal equality, his inability to expose himself to similarly strong egos who stand on a par and who do not feel any sense of subordination, is not only a disadvantage for the president, but a subtle and insidious threat to his comprehension of himself and his problems. For any president, there is significant risk that deference will distort his ability to produce rational decisions and encourage an artificial inflation of his self-concept.

BEHAVIORAL OUTCOMES

Table 2 depicts the patterns of deference from its origin in the symbolic function through its influence on presidential behavior, to which the discussion now turns.

Two kinds of "undesireable"[4] presidential behaviors are encouraged by and can be identified as partial consequences of long-term

Table 2   Patterns of Deference

ROLE DEMAND	INEVITABLE EXPOSURE	PSYCHOLOGICAL MEANING
Symbolic Function	Status inequality: interpersonal encounters	Distorts social comparison processes
PSYCHOLOGICAL EXPERIENCE	CUMULATIVE PSYCHOLOGICAL IMPACT[a]	PRESIDENTIAL BEHAVIOR[a]
Deference: artificially positive feedback	"Inflation of self-concept" distorted perception of external events	"Over-identification" with presidency (e.g., distinction between self and office blurs) Misinformed decisions (e.g., Nixon fires Archibald Cox)

[a]varies with individual differences

exposure to deference. The first can be termed "misinformed decisions": specific, politically significant choices a president makes,
without adequately forecasting the probable consequences. The second is "over-identification" with the presidency, wherein the president, by his word and deed, blurs the distinction between himself
and the institution, shows that his personal identity has merged with
the office he holds, and thereby creates an unhealthy link, in the
minds of citizens, between the fate of the presidency and his fate as
a person. Let us consider first how a climate of excessive deference
encouraged a political decision that so undermined the confidence of
the people that it ultimately drove a duly elected American president
from office.

A CRISIS OF LEGITIMACY: NIXON FIRES COX

In the fall of 1973, the White House was under seige, and Watergate
was the reason.

Mounting public suspicion had dictated that a Special Prosecutor
be named to pursue the investigation wherever it led, including, if

need be, the White House. Nixon's appointment of Archibald Cox to this post had been dictated by the need to insure an independent and legitimate status for the Special Prosecutor. Cox, a liberal, democratic Harvard law professor with ties to the Kennedy family, appeared to fit the bill.

The atmosphere inside the White House was tense and confused. Nixon's behavior throughout the spring and summer of 1973 was in keeping with his reputation as an image-conscious, political manipulator. In his efforts to extricate himself from the widening, poisonous stain that Watergate was becoming, he combined evasive public statements with behind-the-scenes maneuvering. Many long-time Nixon aides were bewildered by Nixon's behavior, uncertain of Nixon's role in the affair, and puzzled at his reluctance to make a clean breast of his involvement. Like much of the rest of the country, they were suspicious, but were still more than willing to give the president the benefit of the doubt.

On the one hand, Nixon's lack of forthrightness was troublesome, and it contributed to a sense of unease, which his people fought to repress. There was a disquieting fear that Nixon was being evasive in order to protect himself from risky consequences of truth.

On the other hand, the strong code of loyalty and support for the president was intensified by the stressfulness of the situation. The incentive system that Nixon had established within his official family had always strongly reinforced soldierly behavior—particularly when the chief was under attack. Devil's advocates and internal critics like Walter Hickel or even Patrick Moynihan had been shown the door. Those who stayed "on the reservation" and were otherwise useful were rewarded (Dean, 1976). Nixon represented himself to his people as a lonely, DeGaulle-like figure, shrouded in mystique, misunderstood and wronged by his enemies throughout his career, yet capable of greatness and worthy of the kind of special fealty reserved for the great. Coupled with the reward structure, this image had long since ensured that the face-to-face counseling that Nixon received from his people would tend to support his self-image and reinforce his own interpretations of events.

The events surrounding the Cox decision would at least temporarily lay any internal suspicions to rest. Cox had been tough and stubborn. And he had succeeded in winning a court order which required Nixon to serve up his tapes. This raised genuine constitutional questions of presidential privilege, which made it easier to view Cox's dogged determination as a politically inspired move to besmirch an old enemy, regardless of the cost to the presidency. This view seemed particularly plausible in light of the volatile situation in the Middle East, which suddenly erupted into the Yom Kippur War.

Nixon was deeply involved in delicate maneuvers aimed at resolving the Middle East crisis. He was convinced that a confrontation with Cox and the courts would severely undermine his credibility in foreign capitals at a time when he felt he desperately needed to speak and act with the moral and military force of the United States solidly behind him. So Nixon proposed a compromise which, to his mind and to the minds of his advisors, was not only fair but essential to the president's credibility on the international stage. A third party, someone Nixon could trust, like Senator John Stennis of Mississippi, would prepare an "authenticated summary" of the contents of the tapes.

When Cox rejected this proposal, Nixon and his aides rigidified. Theodore White (1975) reports that at least five people involved in the deliberations inside the Nixon camp—Alexander Haig, Pat Buchanan, Fred Buzhardt, Leonard Garment, and Charles Alan Wright—felt strongly that Nixon should fire Cox for insubordination. Only Attorney General Elliot Richardson, a longtime friend of Cox, disagreed with this course of action. So, on Saturday, October 20th, 1973, the "Saturday Night Massacre" occurred. Archibald Cox was fired, Elliot Richardson and his Deputy Attorney General William Ruckelshaus resigned, unleashing what Alexander Haig would later call "the day of the firestorm." These events broke the back of the Nixon presidency.

Many important contextual details are missing from this account, but the key question for our purposes has been brought into focus:

How could Nixon and his advisors have failed to anticipate the massive outrage that would follow a decision to fire Archibald Cox?

No reasonably objective and informed observer could have missed predicting that, given the context, such an act would destroy Nixon's moral-symbolic hold on the people. Sure enough, as Theodore White (1975, pp. 342–43) observes:

> The reaction that evening was as near instantaneous as it had been at Pearl Harbor, or the day of John Kennedy's assassination—an explosion as unpredictable and as sweeping as mass hysteria.

Worse, the decision galvanized the national will into a rejection of Nixon's legitimacy as president:

> The question was now not one of burglary, break-in, cover-up, but of power itself—and the White House had been caught in a total misreading of the American mind (White, 1975, p. 345).

It is important that this total misreading was taken by a group that included men whose character and judgment equipped them for much greater accuracy. People like Garment, Wright, or Buchanan are neither sycophants nor fools. They were men who, because of press and isolation, fixed on the view that they were defenders of the presidential institution under attack. Clearly, this was Nixon's best legal defense; but moral, as well as expedient energies lay behind that view. In other words, Nixon's men really believed it. But because the wagons were circled, they failed to appreciate the depth and severity of Nixon's problem with the people. They didn't know what any citizen knew—that such a gross defiance by a man under suspicion would provoke massive outrage and, ultimately, absolute rejection of Nixon as president:

> Isolated in their pockets, hardened by years of press hostility, they had for weeks and months ignored editorials, protests, denunciations, even appeals from within their own party. Now, as the firestorm burst, they could answer to no-one the primary question of everyone: What was the President hiding? (White, 1975, p. 345).

Perceptions in and perceptions outside the White House were sharply divergent. Available accounts of the internal events leading up to the decision suggest that these men honestly felt that there was a chance that enough of the country would see this decision the way the president saw it: as a chief executive protecting his office against an unruly, partisan subordinate in a time of crisis. In fact, the people saw it as a transparent and outrageous ploy: Fabricate a crisis, then evoke the traditions of the presidency to justify firing your problem.

What difference did Nixon's deference patterns make in this episode? Obviously, factors additional to deference were also at work here—the tense international situation, the unrelieved pressure of Watergate, and Nixon's personal proclivities toward aggressive defiance among them. But the deference-saturated internal climate of the Nixon White House laid the foundation for the misperceptions that would produce the Cox decision. Reflexive and worshipful obeisance to the president and the presidency was firmly entrenched long before Watergate. Nixon's picture of external events had always been filtered through a network of fiercely loyal and partisan gatekeepers. The internal incentive system had long since extinguished autonomous, independent, and critical thinking. Nixon's identification with a powerful, dominant, and aggressive presidency had early on been firmly implanted in the minds of his people. If his record meant anything, it was inevitable that Nixon would respond to any serious challenge by flexing the muscles of the presidency. His people anticipated this, and it colored their judgment. And it was equally inevitable that any decision about when and how to use that power would be taken internally, without the benefit of consultation with outsiders—particularly critical outsiders. These facts make it unlikely that Nixon would have tolerated Cox's behavior even if Nixon had had nothing important to lose by surrendering his tapes to the court.

Thus, the events of October, 1973 served only to emphasize and intensify tendencies that were already well established. The Middle East crisis evoked and revitalized Nixon's sense of moral rectitude and presidential vigor. The ongoing Watergate problem had already accentuated the Nixon circle's preoccupation with the issues and nuances surrounding presidential privilege. The Watergate debate had come to be framed in terms of such prerogatives as executive privilege and the right to protect the national security. These things were on everybody's minds when the Cox challenge arose, and in the context of the Yom Kippur War, they assumed a fresh urgency, credence, and moral force. To Nixon's advisors, dismissing Cox had the aura of a righteous and proper act, because Cox was trying to undermine the president at precisely the time when, to their minds, the national interest compelled support for the president.

The long-established pattern of isolation, reinforced by Nixon's management system and intensified by the Watergate ordeal, ensured that these feelings would not be diluted by full appreciation for the deep and abiding suspicion with which the public viewed Richard Nixon by that time. The Nixon men failed to recognize the extent to which Nixon had weakened the psycho-moral bonds between the people and the presidency. They knew there would be cries of outrage and foul play from their already established critics. But incredibly, they expected the "silent majority" to see what they saw and feel what they felt. With this act, Richard Nixon lost any protection his status as president could have afforded him. Temporarily at least, the president lost all legitimacy. And the primary reason for this gross misperception was, I think, the rarified and unreal sense of presidential omnipotence that had been nurtured inside their walled-off camp.

OVERIDENTIFICATION WITH THE PRESIDENCY

As mentioned earlier, overidentification with the presidency describes a situation in which the president, by his word and deed, shows that he has incorporated his job into his sense of who he is. I conceive this to be an undesirable state of affairs because such behavior tends to blur the distinction, in the minds of the people, between the person of the president and his temporary assignment. It forges an unhealthy link between the fate of the presidency and the fate of the person who happens to be president.

This works against the institutional continuity that has usefully characterized the office for most of its history. The office is healthiest when it is collectively viewed as a temporary trust with a stable identity of its own, independent of the succession of.personalities who have held it. By absorbing the colors of only the most illustrious of its incumbents, the presidency has attained that fragile but independent stature that has enabled it to promote political stability and to serve as the fulcrum for the social progress this country has enjoyed. This stature is threatened by the personalization of the presidency.

Deference can foster overidentification by encouraging a president to incorporate the trappings, powers, and prerogatives of office into his self-definition. Observable signs of this state are the behaviors that encourage the link between man and office in the minds of citizens. These behaviors are: unusual interest in and attention to the ceremonial or symbolic trappings of office; preoccupation with the niceties of protocol; special attention to status issues in personal dealings; over-use of the media; and the creation of well-publicized opportunities for emphasizing one's association with the magnificant traditions of the presidency.

Not all presidents fall prey to this tendency. Many, perhaps most, have responded like Harry Truman, for whom the distinction between self and office remained clear and prominent throughout his tenure despite his exposure to deference. This was made manifest by the unadorned lifestyle to which Truman returned upon completing his term. His behavior stands in sharp contrast to the patterns displayed by former presidents Lyndon Johnson and Richard Nixon, both of whom continued to surround themselves with the trappings and the atmosphere of high office.

Again, the clearest example is supplied by Richard Nixon. From his attempt to attire the White House police in resplendent uniforms reminiscent of European palace guards to his exaggeratedly formal sense of presidential dignity, Nixon revealed his fascination with the appointments and perquisites of presidential status. For reasons others have traced to his character and impulse, Nixon seemed desperate to lose himself in the mantle of the presidency (Mazlish,

1972). And this was apparent long before his disastrous attempt to use the office to shield himself from the consequences of Watergate.

The earliest signs were faint. In recounting an exchange between Nixon and an acquaintance in the oval office shortly after his 1968 election, Leonard Lurie (1972, p. 306) provides a glimpse of Nixon's feelings about his relationship to the presidency:

> In a discussion with Nixon about the proper price [of land Nixon sought to purchase in Key Biscayne], Hoke Maroon prefaced his protest with: "But Dick"—only to be cut off by an angry Nixon, who coldly interjected: "Don't you dare call me Dick. I am the President of the United States. When you speak to me you call me Mr. President."

The next sign was clearer, but was clothed in the necessities of the re-election campaign. According to Nixon speechwriter William Safire (1975), it was the low level of voter affection for Nixon the man that prompted the decision to disassociate the Nixon name from campaign promotional activities. The slogan, "Re-elect the President," was, moreover, consistent with the strategy of having Nixon adopt an "above the battle" stance. It is probably even true, as Safire claims, that others, not Nixon, initiated and pushed for the no-name slogan. Yet the departure from custom was so sharp, the posture so quintessentially Nixonian, that it is not unreasonable to interpret this ostensibly political decision in deeper and more personal terms.

For Nixon knew that his style had created a reservoir of mistrust and ill will toward himself all along his path to political success. And despite his frequent protestations that he would rather be respected than loved, those close to him have intimated that he felt cheated of the warm adulation that accomplishments less impressive than his own had won for other men.

Thus, it seems plausible that Nixon sensed a chance to win public acceptance for the new identity he cherished, and public detachment from the old, unloved identity, by means of a media campaign which omitted mention of his name and juxtaposed his familiar face with the lofty title and carefully tailored behavior of the president.

It is a measure of Nixon's success at personalizing the presidency, and a clear indication of the consequences of such a course, that so many analysts at the time saw the Watergate affair as a crisis of the presidency rather than as the crisis of a man who happened to be president. This interpretation has subsided. But it is precisely the kind of confusion that can work irreparable harm to the institutional continuity of the office.

I have relied heavily on the presidency of Richard Nixon to illustrate the two major behavioral consequences of sustained exposure to deference for good reasons: Nixon's behavioral responses were exaggerated. His hunger for the stature of office made him unusually susceptible to the influences of deference, and thus his behavior presents an unusually clearcut example of how such treatment can influence a president. Nixon's inability to see outside his private world at a critical moment—an ability that was nurtured and enlarged by deference throughout his term—very nearly destroyed the legitimacy of the presidency in the eyes of his countrymen. Other examples are available, but they are less pointed. Nixon's reaction is an extreme case, but by no means an isolated case.

Other presidents—those most would judge to be far better suited to the presidency than Nixon—have been encouraged and emboldened by their status into foolish acts.[5] But most important is that our treatment of presidents continues to threaten the accuracy with which they are able to gauge themselves and events, in spite of the mood of reappraisal sparked by Watergate. The institutional sources of encouragement for the behavior described in this chapter remain intact.

Those who take comfort from the presidencies of Arthur, Van Buren, or Truman—men who seemed immune to the headiness of power—need only ask themselves how realistic it is to expect the selection process to produce such presidents consistently and in perpetuity. The prospects, most would agree, are slim. But if indefinite reliance on character is too chancy, what other options are open?

How can the subtly distorting influences of deference be arrested or eliminated?

WHAT CAN BE DONE?

As the early pages of this chapter suggested, the impact of power and status on the powerful is an ancient concern. In the United States, public distaste for presidential royalism dates back to the Federalist era. George Washington's conduct in office was heavily influenced by his formal and stately sense of propriety and station, and this contributed to his decline in popularity in his second term. John Adams was less regal, but equally distant and aloof. And Thomas Jefferson was to enjoy considerable political success with a systematic strategy of de-royalizing the presidency. Jefferson emphasized his "oneness" with the common man, and otherwise conducted himself so as to minimize the status gap between the president and the people. More recently, President Jimmy Carter has successfully employed a similar strategy of humanizing and de-royalizing the presidency. The contrast with the Nixonian penchant for elevated mystique has been refreshing. Carter's "common" touch has been well-received.

The Jefferson and Carter strategies represent the principal solution to the problems of deference that has been tried thus far. Augmented by popular and scholarly literature which takes a critical, revisionist view of the exalted presidency (e.g., Reedy, 1970; Cronin, 1975), such initiatives appear to have been effective in context. They seem to make the point that a president who wishes to do so may, at his own initiative, arrest or at least minimize the influence dynamics described in this chapter.

But this is a temporary solution at best. It depends too heavily on the discretion of presidents—an unpredictable quantity. Not only is his behavior subject to change at will, but his term of office is limited to a maximum of eight years. What happens after that depends on the roll of the electoral dice.

Further, there is a cosmetic quality to such a solution. For however a president chooses to style himself, and whatever the touches of commonness he affects, he retains his singular position of power. Those who deal with him will not lose sight of this fact, and will continue to defer to his judgment, even if in more subtle and less exaggerated ways.

To my mind, continued reliance on presidential discretion as an antidote for the distortions of deference is tantamount to inviting the cyclic re-emergence of deference as a threat to presidential perceptions. For one thing, the Jefferson-Carter strategy rarely springs into existence without encouragement. It usually follows upon a presidency or an era whose practices and excesses provoked widespread disaffection, as well as a clamor for a democratized presidency. Thus, to leave things as they are is to expect and to accept both extremes of the pendulum's path.

The most frequently mentioned solution focuses not on presidential self-help, but on changing the sentiments of citizens. The arguments of Reedy (1970), Schlesinger (1973) and Cronin (1975) point to the need for reshaping citizen attitudes toward and expectations of the presidency and presidents. If only we can muster a little skeptical disrespect toward both on the part of the people, presidents will be exposed to less obeisance, will give themselves fewer airs, will be more attuned to reality, and will make fewer poor decisions. Though it has merit, the problem with this solution is that it, too, is ultimately temporary and transitory. It does not reflect appreciation for the fact that citizens need an anthropomorphic symbol of government, and that they will—in the long run—tend to idealize that human symbol. Americans already anchor a deep-rooted strain of fear and mistrust of government power. Yet this has historically been insufficient to sustain a truly skeptical view of the presidency. Yes, we can imbue this generation of Americans with greater skepticism. Indeed, events have already done so. It might even be wise to institute such supportive practices as a legislative question period, at which presidents could be treated with the same irreverence now accorded British, Canadian, or Israeli prime ministers. But sustaining that skepticism would require—paradoxically—a steady recurrence of presidential abuses, the very thing we seek to avoid. In troubled times, the yearning for the reassurance of a human authority figure would resurface and intensify the president's exposure to citizen idealizations, thus rekindling the influence dynamics that have been described. The cultivation of popular skepticism can only be a partial solution, then, because it promises to be a temporary one.

Two potential structural reforms deserve mention, although neither is likely to be adopted for a variety of reasons. The first would remove much of the president's exposure to deference by detaching the symbolic function from the presidency. Symbolic responsibilities would be invested in a new station, say, a Chancellor of the United States, analogous to the British monarch. This would permit the presidency to assume a businesslike, relatively colorless workaday air, divorced from the pretensions and pomposities of symbolic statecraft. Presidents would no longer have any reason to regard themselves as embodiments of the majesty of the United States government. As nothing more than the managing director of government, a president would be much freer from the distortions of deference. Such a solution is alluring, but poses nearly insurmountable problems of its own. It would require a constitutional amendment and a massive citizen reorientation program—both of which bode ill for any chance of acceptance.

Another possibility would be to give the president true peers— colleagues who felt free to tell him to "go soak his head." But this would involve more than simply requiring the president to consult with the Senate Foreign Relations Committee, as Rexford Tugwell (1974) has suggested. Nor does it mean the creation of a small "executive council," comprised of distinguished citizens, with which the president must consult, but whose advice he is free to ignore, as Benjamin V. Cohen (1974) has proposed. To arrest the influence dynamics described in this chapter effectively, it would be necessary to give the president formal and equally powerful peers; to make him share his executive mantle; to create absolute status equality among a group of co-equal presidents. Such a reform would accomplish its objective by reintroducing social comparison processes anchored more firmly in a shared reality. But it has no chance of attainment. Like the Chancellor idea, it is an intriguing option that could represent a dramatic solution to status inequality; but it is an option which is not likely to be put to the test.

Again, we are forced back on character as the most likely recourse. Character is the domain most accessible and potentially most responsive to our efforts to improve things. Despite the lack of any widely accepted or demonstrably effective technology for assessing personality, the apparent absence of viable alternatives suggests we must learn to spot those—like Arther, Van Buren, or Truman—who can remain relatively unspoiled by celebratory treatment. But before looking closely and carefully at character in Chapter 7, we must consider two additional challenges to character posed by the presidential experience. Frustration, the classic experience of democratic leadership, is the subject of Chapter 6. Dissonance—the lure of expedient misrepresentation—concerns us next.

NOTES

1. See Note 3, Chapter 1.

2. Lyndon Johnson's treatment of his aides in such situations was overtly coercive. As Barber (1977, p. 82) observes: The President would bring together a small group and get consent by polling each in turn. Senator Fulbright, Chester Cooper, and others have recalled the intimidating effect of this technique of Johnson's, standard as it is. Apparently it worked this way. In 1967 Secretary McNamara's doubts about the value of more war in Vietnam were escalating. Meeting with the President and the generals, McNamara faced this situation.

   "The troops that General Westmoreland needs and requests, as we feel it necessary, will be supplied," Johnson said, then asked, "Is that not true, General Westmoreland?"
   "I agree, Mr. President."
   "General Wheeler?"
   "That is correct, Mr. President."
   "Secretary McNamara?"
   "Yes, sir," came a helpless reply.

3. Two of Barber's low self-esteem categories, the active-negative (e.g., Wilson, Nixon) and the passive-positive (e.g., Taft, Harding), seem

especially likely to invite such treatment. The hunger of the first for power, and the second for love, suggest unusual susceptibility to supportive, favorable, and confirming feedback. Active-positives (e.g., JFK, FDR) and passive-negatives (e.g., Eisenhower, Coolidge) seem less susceptible; the first because of character-rooted self-sufficiency, the second because of a penchant for aloofness and detachment. But no one is totally impervious to such treatment.

4. The identification of such behaviors as "undesirable" involves, of course, a value judgment on my part. Let this footnote serve as my statement of the value bases for the personal judgments that riddle these pages. As I make apparent in Chapter 8, I conceive of three value bases for judging presidential behavior. The first, which I believe to have temporal priority over the others, pertains to the value of political stability, order, and survival. When the president behaves in a way that threatens the stability or legitimacy of the political order (e.g., Nixon's Watergate evasions, Ford's pardon of Nixon), or the physical safety of the country or its inhabitants (e.g., Kennedy's refusal to "back down" during the Cuban Missile Crisis), such behavior can be termed "undesirable." Legitimacy, stability, and safety are threatened when the president risks war, or when his actions undermine the people's faith and trust in governmental arrangements. In systems-theory terms, the highest value is system survival in recognizable form (Von Bertalanffy, 1968). The second value base is democratic. When the president shows blatant disregard for the rights of individual citizens (e.g., Nixon and Daniel Ellsberg), groups (e.g., FDR's incarceration of Japanese-Americans during World War II), other nations (e.g., Polk's provocation of war with Mexico as a pretext for acquiring Texas and California), or constitutional processes (e.g., use of the military without congressional approval), such behavior is appropriately labeled "undesirable" on moral-democratic grounds. Third is performance effectiveness. When the president or the presidency can be shown to be performing one or another of the generic functions (see Chapter 2) in an inefficient or ineffective manner, as indicated by realistic performance criteria (see H.A. Simon, 1945, pp. 172–197), such performance is justly termed "undesirable" (e.g., the apparent failure of the presidency and various presidents to forecast the energy crisis adequately, and to mobilize a program and political support to cope with it). In sum, presidential behavior is "undesirable" when it is dangerous, morally wrong, or doesn't work. However undesirable, I

recognize that such behavior may nonetheless be judged as necessary or inevitable in context by contemporary observers. Finally, both of the behaviors discussed in the text, "misinformed decisions" and "overidentification" with the presidency, are illustrated with examples that involved significant threats to system survival. But other examples involving threats to the other values could be adduced as well.

5. Take, for example, Theodore Roosevelt, whose arrogant and baldly illegal acquisition of the Panama Canal zone is attributable to an exalted sense of presidential prerogative. Historian Henry Pringle (1956) writes of the self-delusionary quality of Roosevelt's rationale for an act that remains a blight on U.S.–Latin American relations to this day. For additional examples of the impact of exalted conceptions of the presidency on presidents' foreign policy decisions, see Schlesinger (1973).

Our presidents have established, by precedent, that they and members of their Cabinet have an undoubted privilege and discretion to keep confidential, in the public interest, papers and information which require secrecy.

WOLKINSON, *"Demands of Congressional Committees for Executive Papers"*

As we have seen, it is a recurring fact of presidential life, to become entangled in circumstances in which the president has much at stake, and, from his point of view, much to lose. It is also a fact, as the testimony of past presidents bears witness, that the power resources of the job rarely seem equal to its demands. As Emmet John Hughes (1972, p. 169) puts it:

> . . .All of them, from the most venturesome to the most reticent, have shared one disconcerting experience: the discovery of the limits and restraints—decreed by law, by history and by circumstance—that sometimes can blur their clearest designs or dull their sharpest purposes.

DISSONANCE:
The Lure
Of Expediency

5

A president who plays strictly by the rules puts himself at an enormous disadvantage. If he is to work his will and put his personal stamp on outcomes, he must somehow find a way to circumvent the seemingly endless limits that hinder his discretion. As the next chapter argues, the obstacles that are repeatedly thrust into his path serve as incentives in their own right—motivating openly aggressive and intemperate behavior. The purpose of the present chapter, however, is to make the point that the presidency has an underlife. The tension between the demands of office and the limits of power may well produce baldfaced, above-board presidential aggression. But it is equally possible, as this chapter shows, that such tension will drive the president underground to seek the line of least resistance in expedient misrepresentation as the surest way to work his will.

ORIGINS: ADVOCATE AND SYMBOLIC FUNCTIONS

One reason they lie is that their duties accustom them to certain kinds of misrepresentation as a matter of course. Presidents experience constant pressure, both subtle and unsubtle, to misrepresent themselves to their various constituencies. This is inherent in the symbolic and policy advocate functions. Symbolically, presidents are expected to embody our important values and to "inspire our betterness" (Barber, 1977). As the spiritual and ceremonial leader of the nation, the president is enjoined to speak and act accordingly. This expectation puts pressure on the president to construct and represent himself along certain lines for our benefit. For most, this has implied an effort to speak and act in ways consistent with all the noble but mythical qualities that citizens attribute to presidents.

Misrepresentation results from the fact that presidents, as human beings, possess full measures of the kinds of human failings which, if revealed, would seem inconsistent with their symbolic status. Thus, many have found it necessary to de-emphasize warts, to give the appearance of decisiveness when it is in fact absent, and to acknowledge only the purest of motives, even when impure motives are operating. Presidential peccadillos, like John Kennedy's, Eisenhower's, or FDR's extramarital activities; presidential pain and self-doubt, such as that expressed by Warren G. Harding in connection with his tax reform problem (see p. 38); or such unlovely incidents from the president's past as LBJ's alleged election fraud in Texas, are routinely shielded from the public's eyes. They become generally known, if at all, only after the president has departed the office and the earth. Even the press tacitly colludes in the suppression of much such information, on the grounds that behavior like this (excepting, of course, such things as election-rigging) does not bear directly on the public interest.

Politically, the president is encouraged to misrepresent for different reasons. The symbolic president seeks to inspire, but the political president must sell both his programs and his party. As a partisan advocate, he is bound to present his case in the best possible light. This often means that he will seek credit for accomplishments that are not really his, that he will shift the blame for his mistakes onto the shoulders of others, and that he will rarely or never admit anything that would cast his administration into an unflattering light. For a wickedly perceptive treatment of this cynical side of the presidency, see Thomas Cronin's discussion of the "Presidency Public Relations Script" in Tugwell and Cronin (1974: 168–83).

His symbolic and advocacy functions thus *accustom* the president to misrepresenting himself. They *condition* him to deceive. As his symbolic and advocacy experience accumulates, he becomes more familiar with dissembling and more comfortable with its use.

Augmenting this process of familiarization is the fact that presidents operate in a morally flexible milieu. By longstanding custom, they are freer than anyone else to ignore or redefine traditional moral dictums, if only because, as Emmet John Hughes (1972, pp. 129–30) puts it:

> The most innovative and effective Presidents, from the start of the Republic, have been those most ready, at any propitious moment, to break their own unbreakable commandments of the past.

The political professionals who comprise the president's occupational reference group typically expect and encourage him to exploit this freedom to his personal and political advantage. And students of the presidency are nearly unanimous in acknowledging that un-scrupulousness and moral opaqueness of various kinds is to be expected of presidents, particularly successful ones (see Hess, 1974; Hughes, 1972). In the words of historian Thomas A. Bailey (1966, p. 140):

> Now the President must reveal shrewdness and cleverness—cunning not unmixed with guile. Indeed, except for the bedazzlement of an occasional military hero like Eisenhower, he can hardly reach his high office, much less stay there, unless he is something of a political manipulator. Martin Van Buren was so adroit that he honestly won such titles as the American Talleyrand, the Little Magician. . . . His enemies charged that he rowed toward his objectives with "muffled oars."

There is thus an implicit climate of tolerance surrounding the presidency—a tolerance which has countenanced presidential liberties with the truth for most of the country's history. This climate is nourished and sustained, of course, by the long-established tradition of presidential secrecy in the interests of national security, encapsuled in the statement by Herman Wolkinson that opened this chapter. In a thoroughgoing review of recent governmental deception and secrecy, David Wise (1973, p. 503) argues that a "right to lie" norm pervades not only the presidency, but the highest policy councils as well:

> In its baldest terms, this philosophy has been stated as the "right to lie." The elite policy makers have. . .found an easy justification for both deception and secrecy. They are the only ones who "read the cables" and the intelligence reports and "have the information." Ordinary citizens, they believe, cannot understand complex foreign policy problems; ergo, the policy makers have the right, so they think, to mislead the public for its own good.

Thus we see that the vectors of influence—his symbolic and advocacy functions, the tradition of pragmatic guile, and the norms that pervade the upper reaches of government—all serve to encourage presidents to see the control of at least some kinds of information as not just expedient, but as essential and legitimate political resources, a rationale in their minds as they confront their choices.

THE EXPOSURE: TEMPTATION

The rub comes, however, when the president is tempted to transfer his acquired attitudes and behaviors beyond the symbolic and advocacy realms into his other problem areas, particularly those where his personal status is threatened. Since his knowledgeable critics fully expect him to cross lines that others rarely cross, and since he is the sole judge of the morality of his behavior before the fact, the president is left to experience a variety of situational temptations in the absence of the kinds of social, interpersonal, and moral constraints that inhibit the actions of others.[1]

Any president is repeatedly embroiled in morally complex dilemmas, public disclosure of which would surely tarnish, at least in the short run, the symbolic stature which underlies his political power. And, as was noted at the outset of this chapter, strict adherence to the "rules of the game" will, as often as not, seem equivalent to surrendering any hopes the president has of working his will against the forces of opposition. Given how he has been socialized, and given the inevitable emergence of situations in which straightforward honesty will seem tantamount to presidential surrender, it is obvious and inevitable that a threatened president will be tempted by the lure of expedient misrepresentation.

PSYCHOLOGICAL EXPERIENCE: COGNITIVE DISSONANCE

As matters stand, the only effective constraint on presidential lying is internal to the president.[2] Cognitive psychologists argue that there is an innate human need for consistency between thought and action, word and deed. Leon Festinger (1957) has demonstrated that when subjects are experimentally induced to speak and act in ways inconsistent with their private sentiments or knowledge, they experience extreme discomfort and display strong motivation to reduce the inconsistency, either by renouncing their behavior, or by adjusting their attitudes and perceptions into consistency with the dissonant behavior. For those presidents whose private sentiments include strong moral strictures against lying and misrepresentation, the consistency drive may well act as a significant internal check. For example, Harry Truman's private moral code appears largely responsible for a presidential record almost entirely free from any systematic use of deceit. But why doesn't the need for cognitive consistency serve as an important internal barrier against lying for any president? One reason, of course, is that some presidents feel little internal compunction against misrepresenting themselves.[3] If there are no internal sentiments standing in opposition to deceit, deceitful behavior will not give rise to dissonance.

Another reason, as psychologist Elliot Aronson (1972) points out, is that there is a third way (other than renouncing one's behavior, or changing one's mind) to resolve the unpleasant sensations of cognitive dissonance: recourse to an external justification. Most presidents, one might guess, experience some twinge of guilt—the kind of physical response a lie-detector would record—which suggests dissonance. But if there is good reason to lie, the internal pain of lying can be avoided by recourse to the justification. And as we have noted, presidents have many, perhaps too many, sources of external justification readily at hand. The moral freedom of the office, the tacit expectation that it will be used, the "right to lie" norm, the ease with which rubrics like "national security" or "the public interest" can be used to legitimize deceit, or the need to prevent loss of respect for the presidency, are among these external justifications.

Since presidents are constantly confronted with sensitive political and moral dilemmas, since the line of least resistance in their resolution will often be misrepresentation in one form or another, and since justificatory rationales are readily at hand, lying is a frequently employed presidential stratagem. There is evidence to suggest that presidents *routinely* employ "mystification and deception" in their dealings with the press and in times of major political crisis. Political psychologist Henry Alker (1976), using a technique developed by the Linguistic Society of America, assessed the extent of deception employed in press conferences by presidents Eisenhower, Kennedy, Johnson, Nixon, and Ford. The results suggested that each of these men dissembled in some way when dealing with the press, and that deception was most pronounced during periods of important political crisis. The results also showed that Nixon was the most deceiving, followed by Kennedy, Ford, Johnson, and Eisenhower, in that order.

The variety of character types in this list is a strong argument against the assumption that none of these presidents felt any scruples against lying in general. The more plausible interpretation is that most of them felt justified, in terms of one or another of the rationales mentioned earlier, in misrepresenting themselves. But despite the ready availability of justification, it is clear that their circumstances guarantee that presidents in general will repeatedly experience varying intensities of cognitive dissonance. Internal scruples will continuously come into conflict with situational temptations and incentives in the course of a presidential term. And since a recurring stimulus eventually produces a conditioned response, the question then arises: What conditioned responses emerge from recurring presidential exposure to dissonance?

CUMULATIVE PSYCHOLOGICAL IMPACTS

Two possibilities, both implicit in Festinger's theory of cognitive dissonance, suggest themselves. The first, and seemingly the most common, can be termed an "erosion" of truth norms.

The pressure to lie touches the president's personal value system. His response in any given situation depends on the importance of truth values to his self-definition, relative to the importance of ends that would be served by misrepresentation. As noted, situational temptations are characteristically strong, and offer easy rationales for deceptive behavior. In the context of such circumstances, biblical or parental conceptions of honesty are easily dismissed as naive, unrealistic, and irrelevant.

As the temptations accumulate, and as the number of situational surrenders to temptation grows, it is likely that the president will develop a facility for rationalization that increases in strength like a well-exercised muscle. This process explains, I think, the routine "mystification and deception" uncovered by Alker's study of presidential press conferences. At least in connection with expedient and readily justified deception, cognitive consistency is no longer experienced as a need. In this manner the pressure to lie can work a cumulative effect describable as an "erosion" of truth norms.

In this pattern of internal adjustment to cognitive dissonance, the president is aware that he is lying, but feels that it is amply justified. In the second form to be described, the need for cognitive consistency continues to operate, but in the direction of altering the president's perceptions of reality. That is, he may block out inconsistent or disconfirming evidence, or otherwise adjust his perception of external events to render them consistent with his misrepresenting pronouncements (Smith, 1973).

Such an adaptation begins with a calculated untruth, told in the interests of expediency or in the genuine belief that it is necessary and wise in terms of some higher value. Then, if the president is forced to confront disconfirming evidence or public charges that he has dissembled, and if he meets these charges with repeated public insistences that his version rather than his critics' is the accurate one, a process psychologists call *behavioral commitment* may be set into motion. Charles Kiesler (1971) poses five conditions under which behavior or utterance can shape commitment to consistent attitudes or beliefs:

1. When the behavior is explicit, public, and unambiguous;
2. When the behavior is important for the subject;
3. When the subject perceives the behavior as irrevocable;
4. When the subject repeats the behavior frequently;
5. When the subject perceives himself to be acting volitionally.

A clear illustration is offered by Richard Nixon's behavior and pronouncements in the Watergate affair. We cannot be certain of Nixon's private assessment of his own culpability at the time of his
first public assertion of his innocence, but the evidence suggests that
he knew himself to be distorting reality at that time—probably for
what he believed to be the wholly justifiable purpose of disassociating the presidency from foolish and illegitimate political activity he
had not directly sanctioned. There is little question that Nixon ascribed great importance to disassociating the presidency from the
incident. And the act was irrevocable in that he certainly had no intention, at that time or later, of backtracking on his insistence that
the White House was not involved. Further, he made repeated public statements insisting that he was innocent of any involvement.
Only the fifth point, volition, is of dubious relevance. Nixon probably did not feel at liberty to change his position after his first public
statement. Indeed, the White House transcripts show him to have
rejected the "hang-out" route time after time. The record shows
many small modifications in his public position. But as late as his
television address announcing the release of the transcripts, he still
insisted that they were consistent with his previous statements, and
that he had told the truth throughout.

A plausible interpretation is that Nixon, throughout this process
of irrevocable commitment, actually came to believe what he was
saying. He was no doubt aware of and privately accepted responsibility for minor untruths which were easy for him to justify. But on
the major points of his honor and his moral responsibility, which
came under sustained critical attack, he appeared to have truly convinced himself of his innocence, despite the embarrassing richness
of contradictory evidence.

This was certainly selective perception. And by the time of his
resignation he had made such a heavy emotional investment in his
public posture (witness his address to the White House staff on the
day of his departure) that his ability to recognize and accept moral
responsibility for the dilemma was questionable.

Unlike rationalization, this form of adjustment to dissonance
moves beyond calculated misrepresentation into the realm of self-

delusion. It is most likely to occur when a president allows himself to be forced into a public posture he later senses to have serious moral or ethical consequences. Unable to accept responsibility for these, he falls prey to a combination of rationalization and behavioral commitment—and resolves the dissonance by adjusting the only aspect of the situation that remains pliable: his mind.

BEHAVIORAL OUTCOMES

Table 3 displays the patterns of dissonance that have been described. In regard to behavioral outcomes, it has been shown that presidents respond to temptation by lying—in small and large ways—while in office. I have acknowledged that much presidential deception is defensible and legitimate, involving the necessary control of national security information, tactful consideration for the feelings of others (see McFarland, 1969), symbolic and advocacy posturing, or the suppression of personal secrets justifiably kept from the public's awareness.

Table 3 Patterns of Dissonance

ROLE DEMAND	INEVITABLE EXPOSURE	PSYCHOLOGICAL MEANING
Policy advocate symbol	Temptation to misrepresent	Personal scruples against lying challenged by temptation
PSYCHOLOGICAL EXPERIENCE	CUMULATIVE PSYCHOLOGICAL IMPACT[a]	PRESIDENTIAL BEHAVIOR[a]
Cognitive dissonance	Erosion of truth norms	Lying, misrepresentation, e.g., Polk and the Mexican War, LBJ and the
	self-delusion	Vietnam War, Nixon and Watergate

[a]varies with individual differences

But what of the consequences of presidential lying? Clearly the presidency encourages presidents to lie, yet much if not most such lying can be readily justified and is widely accepted. What kinds of presidential deception, then, can be labeled "dangerous" or "undesirable," and why?[4]

My answer is that certain kinds of presidential deception—notably that which contravenes basic American ideological tenets; serves no publicly valued, compensatory end; or involves significant costs and sacrifices on the part of citizens—is undesirable because it threatens to undermine the legitimacy of the presidency and the government in the eyes of citizens, once it is revealed to them.[5] A government that is not accepted as legitimate by its citizens is an inherently unstable government (Huntington, 1968). Legitimacy—the generalized belief that government is ethically and morally right and proper—is thus a precious commodity. Political analysts from Plato to Machiavelli to Walter Lippmann have argued that it must be cultivated, nurtured, and constantly revalidated by political leaders who seek to protect their institutions. Yet legitimacy is wrought from a fragile and changeable source: human feelings and sentiments. Feelings are subject to abrupt and dramatic shifts. As Richard Nixon's ill-fated decision to fire Archibald Cox makes unarguably clear, the bedrock of support for a president may vanish overnight. Or, as in the case that follows, legitimacy sentiments may be eroded, in piecemeal fashion, by the emergence of a "credibility gap" between the people and a president.

LYNDON JOHNSON'S VIETNAM

A clear illustration of the influence-dynamics described in this chapter is afforded by Lyndon Johnson's orchestration of the Vietnam war. Apropos of Table 3 (see p. 85), the story begins with a president's policy ambitions. Like most ambitious presidents, Johnson aspired to aims that conflicted in important ways.

His highest priority was to establish himself in history as the architect of the Great Society. In the early years of the Johnson administration, as in only two other twentieth century presidencies (Wilson's and FDR's), special circumstances converged to produce a readiness for dramatic change quite beyond the usual pattern of glacial, incremental change. The trauma of Kennedy's assassination, the civil rights movement, an emerging sensitivity to the scourge of poverty, lessened tensions with the Soviets, and a relatively bright economic picture combined to make possible a massive program of social reform. Johnson had maneuvered brilliantly to win Congressional approval for welfare, civil rights, and education legislation which had been throttled during previous Democratic administrations. Following upon these successes was a reputation for presidential efficacy and legislative wizardry almost without peer in history. This was Johnson's pride and joy, and he was determined to sustain and enlarge upon it.

Set against this stunningly successful program of presidential action was an increasingly ominous threat: the war in Vietnam. Lyndon Johnson did not initiate but rather inherited the premises on which the United States based its commitment to South Vietnam. These had evolved over a period of more than twenty years and three previous presidencies. The experiences of World War II, the evolution of a "cold war" with the Soviet Union, the fear of Munich-like appeasement in the face of an international communist conspiracy—all had contributed to a policy of resistance and containment, of which Vietnam was but the latest expression.

In early 1965, the United States involvement was still largely confined to an "advisory" role in Vietnam. But the war was going badly. It was becoming increasingly apparent that the U.S. position would be compromised unless some action were taken. Johnson was anxious about the war, and felt less confident of his expertise in foreign than in domestic affairs. He was dependent on advice, perhaps more so than any recent American president (Janis, 1972), and his advisers were calling for action.

Johnson knew that some action was required, yet he feared its consequences for his domestic policy initiatives. Whatever action he might take, he was determined not to let the war erode the momentum he had generated behind his Great Society. As he put it (quoted in Kearns, 1976, p. 252):

Oh, I could see it coming all right. History provided too many cases where the sound of the bugle put an immediate end to the hopes and dreams of the best reformers: The Spanish-American War drowned the populist spirit; World War I ended Woodrow Wilson's New Freedom; World War II brought the New Deal to a close. Once the war began, then all those conservatives in Congress would use it as a weapon against the Great Society.

Yet Johnson was equally determined not to "cut and run" in Vietnam (quoted in Kearns, 1976, p. 253):

> . . .Everything I knew about history told me that if I got out of Vietnam and let Ho Chi Minh run through the streets of Saigon, then I'd be doing exactly what Chamberlain did in World War II. I'd be giving a big fat reward to aggression. And I knew that if we let Communist aggression succeed in taking over South Vietnam, there would follow in this country an endless national debate—a mean and destructive debate—that would shatter my presidency, kill my administration, and damage our democracy. I knew that Harry Truman and Dean Acheson had lost their effectiveness from the day that the Communists took over in China. I believed that the loss of China had played a large role in the rise of Joe McCarthy. And I knew that all these problems, taken together, were chickenshit compared with what might happen in Vietnam.

With the communists winning the war, the situation was, Johnson felt, a threat to the international prestige of the United States. He had to make it clear that the U.S. Government had the "will and force and patience and determination" to stay the course and take the necessary action. So, backed by the unanimous support of his foreign policy advisers, Johnson decided to escalate U.S. involvement by bombing the North Vietnamese.

It was Johnson's hope that the bombing would enable him to keep U.S. troop involvements to a minimum, simultaneously minimizing the attention paid by the American people to the conflict. Yet as the bombing wore on, the North Vietnamese continued to prevail. It was increasingly obvious that bombs were not enough. If he was to avoid a collapse of the military effort, Johnson reasoned, it would be necessary to use American troops—not in small numbers as advisers—but in progressively larger numbers as combatants.

By July of 1965 the bombing had been in progress for five months, and the situation had reached crisis proportions. Johnson and his foreign policy group concurred that a full-scale military effort was essential. Yet as they confronted the critical question of how to characterize the decision to the American people, Johnson and most of his advisers parted company.

Johnson's people urged him to go to the Congress, declare a state of emergency, and put the economy on a wartime footing. But Johnson felt certain that a traditional, full-scale mobilization—with the president calling up the reserves and asking the people to sacrifice their money and their sons—would sound the death knell of the Great Society. He knew that a military mobilization was essential to avoid failure in Vietnam, and he was committed to that course. Yet he could not bring himself to sacrifice his domestic dreams by summoning the nation to war. As he struggled with his conflicting aims, it became increasingly clear to him that only one course of action could enable him to have it both ways. He had to deceive the Congress and the American people.

Thus did Lyndon Johnson, tempted beyond his power to resist by what to him were noble and worthy ends, embark upon a course of systematic and large-scale deception. Kiesler's behavioral commitment process was set into motion. Caught as he was between irreconcilable aims that left him no room to maneuver, he fell back on the only political resource left to him: the tradition of presidential control over national security information. Because the president has no peers, because presidents are expected and encouraged to be guileful, because the president can monopolize the sources of foreign policy information, and because presidents are traditionally free to decide such questions themselves, there were no effective external constraints capable of arresting or reversing this decision once Johnson had made it. The circumstances of the presidency first encouraged, and then enabled Johnson to use surreptitious means to work his will.

The specific instances of misrepresentation were numerous. The true cost of the mobilization was hidden in the Defense Department budget, thereby avoiding the danger of alerting Congress via sudden increases in appropriations requests. Troop increases were obtained by extending enlistments and increasing draft calls rather than by mobilizing the reserves. Announcements of impending troop departures were softened by sandwiching them in between other, routine announcements. The administration refused to support needed tax increases, thus sidestepping the possibility of alerting the public to the true state of affairs. Administration officials were vague and evasive in their public statements about the war and its costs. And the Chief Spokesman, Lyndon Johnson, repeatedly described the progress of the war in roseate and optimistic terms, ignoring or suppressing evidence to the contrary. All the while, hundreds of thousands of American troops and billions of dollars in war material were being exported to Vietnam. But for a time, the president was able to sustain the public impression of a limited and controlled war which did not conflict with the domestic ambitions of the administration.

If we can assume that Johnson experienced dissonance—the unpleasant state which precedes rationalization or self-delusion—as a result of the contrast between his public utterance and his private knowledge, how did he resolve it? Initially, it seems, via rationalization. The values of continuing the Great Society and of avoiding the spread of communism were simply more important than the competing value of straightforward honesty. Johnson felt that his use of the secrecy resource would enable the country to realize hard-to-reconcile aims both of which were important to its long-term welfare, and that this success would oblige history and historians to vindicate his judgment.

As the public gradually became aware of the true state of affairs in Vietnam, and as the criticism, disaffection, and discussion of a "credibility gap" appeared and began to mount, there is evidence that Johnson began to display the patterns of behavioral commitment and self-delusion described earlier. Military spending had created serious economic inflation. The media coverage of the war dramatized and clarified the extent of American involvement in

Vietnam. And the war continued to go poorly, even as citizens were treated to a consistent barrage of presidential cheerleading. It became politically acceptable, and increasingly fashionable, to criticize Johnson's performance. Worse still, the Great Society was disintegrating under Congressional pressure, Johnson's popularity was declining precipitously, and the peace movement was gathering momentum. Johnson was forced to watch the things he dreaded most become realities. This was tremendously difficult for him to accept and it galvanized various self-protective distortions. Doris Kearns (1976, pp. 312, 394) describes Johnson's state of mind:

> Deprived of an atmosphere of public support, beseiged at home and abroad, Johnson retreated more and more into the world of his imagination, directing an increasing part of his energies to the task of protecting himself.

Furthermore:

> Most of Johnson—the outer man, the spheres of conscious thought and action—remained intact, for most of the time. But in some ways, increasingly obvious to his close associates, he began to crumble; the suspicions congenital to his nature became delusions; *calculated deceit became self-deception*, and then matters of unquestioned belief. The President's will, once expressed, was not challenged. Advisers began to anticipate his reactions before they said or did anything; self-deceptions multiplied in this hall of distorting mirrors [emphasis mine].

Johnson's self-deception apparently took two forms. The first, which may be likened to Nixon's reaction to Watergate, was to cling to the belief that his interpretation of the progress of the war was accurate, and the second, related form, was to suspect and privately impugn the motives of those who disagreed with him.[6] Furthermore, he abandoned his previous hunger for information, sequestered himself inside the White House, and gradually excised the doubters from his staff. The Tuesday lunch group, which was the central forum for war policy-making, often degenerated into a stage on which Johnson vented his emotions and revealed his delusions (Kearns, 1976, p. 322):

> The constant encouragement he demanded deadened the critical faculties of those still allowed access, creating a *vacuum* around himself and making him a prisoner of his own propaganda. Screening out options, facts, and ideas, Lyndon Johnson's personality operated to distort the truth in much the same way as ideology works in a totalitarian society [emphasis mine].

Johnson's lack of candor with the people, his failure to heed the advice of those who urged him to go to the Congress and the country with his war plans, ultimately destroyed his legitimacy and his presidency.[7] It was not untruthfulness *per se* but untruthfulness about the cost in American lives and money that eroded his support. The people were encouraged to develop inflated expectations that could not be fulfilled. When the realities of war abroad, and of inflation and discord at home, became apparent to them, Johnson's credibility as the national spokesman finally evaporated. He was the focal point for the disenchantment, the man responsible for dead sons, devalued paychecks, and military escapades that were in important respects contrary to basic American ideological tenets.[8] Despite truly impressive legislative successes and other flashes of political brilliance, Johnson's orchestration of the Vietnam war contributed to a serious weakening of the psychological bond between the people and the presidency, which, further weakened by Watergate, has yet to be restored to previous levels of strength.[9]

WHAT CAN BE DONE?

As matters stand, the president alone can determine when and whether to employ deception as a political or personal resource. I have argued, in this and other chapters, that presidents are influenced—by the functions they perform and the exposures they encounter—in ways that predispose them to fall back on this resource, particularly when other options seem closed to them. Though we have elected presidents who in retrospect seemed immune to the temptation, my argument is that any lone ego, beset by constraints, confronting the possibility of failing to achieve the aims he has set for himself and for his generation, yet possessed of the station and the powers of the presidency, is very likely to use deceit in the service of his power stakes. It is simply not realistic to expect a human being, thus positioned and thus tempted, to risk failure or defeat on matters of great importance to him, solely on the grounds of his personal sense of moral or ethical propriety.[10] To depend on this and to occasionally stake the viability and stability of the political system on it is extremely risky. Yet depend on it we must.

The reason is that there is no practical, politically feasible way to prevent presidential deception. Since presidents police themselves before the fact, and since they are subject to restraint only after the undesirable consequences of their behavior become apparent, our best hope must remain the selection of presidents with internalized constraints against lying—personal values and moral codes that inhibit such behavior. The nature of such internal constraints is considered in Chapter 7.

But since even the strongest and most exemplary among us could be seduced by the kind of situation faced by Lyndon Johnson— since decent, psychologically healthy people will occasionally succumb to temptation—we are well advised to identify the external constraints that can supplement character as a check on deception.

Existing constraints depend primarily on the threat of political or legal punishment for the culprits. An outraged citizenry might turn the lying rascals out, as they did Johnson and Nixon, and elect a new man, who, chastened by the excesses of his predecessors, emphasizes honesty and decency in government—as has Jimmy Carter, and, ironically, Nixon before him. The cycle thus repeats itself: discovery, housecleaning, expiation, and renewal. This can improve things. Carter succeeded in improving the government's reputation for openness, trust, and morality—at least for a time.[11] Gerald Ford had a similar impact. But the cycle is activated by deception, and relies upon evidence of further deceit to be reactivated.

Citizen indignation and vigilance depend heavily on fresh evidence of presidential abuses. Since Nixon and Johnson have been the only presidents forced from office essentially because of the untruths they fostered, the potential deterence value of punished presidents cannot yet be thoroughly assayed. We do know that Johnson's fate did not deter Nixon from misleading us.

I think it would be a mistake to rely too heavily on the examples of presidents we have caught at it. To do so is to leave intact the influence vectors that encourage deception, and which virtually guarantee its recurrence. Under present arrangements, we can expect the cycle to continue its course. And it is a sad but safe prediction that future presidents will lie to us—in ways that could prove as harmful and destructive as the deceptions of Johnson and Nixon.

What might be done, then, to supplement our current reliance on character and the threat of punishment? Are there realistic reforms that could prevent or at least strongly discourage presidential deception? Are there ways to remove the incentives which encourage it? Short of a massive, politically unrealistic structural overhaul—such as would be involved in implementing a plural presidency—two less drastic but still potent measures might win political acceptance.

First, we might force presidents to submit to vigorous, unrestricted cross-examination on any aspect of their performance in office. If presidents were required—under oath—to submit themselves to orderly and systematic cross-examination by members of Congress; if normal dignities and courtesies were suspended, so that presidents were treated like any witness under oath; if the president was denied the right to control the scheduling or the format of such examination sessions; if the president—with appropriate safeguards—was denied the right to refuse to answer on national security grounds, it would be far more difficult than it now is to sustain deception on a grand scale, and it would be far less tempting as an expedient solution to otherwise intractible presidential problems.

A second, related possibility would be intense, government and society-wide efforts to create enduring norms of government openness and candor. This would have to be something more than a mere public relations effort. It would first require that much more stringent legal limits be imposed on bureaucratic or presidential secrecy by Act of Congress, as David Wise (1973) has suggested. It would next require a series of sympathetic, committed presidents, willing to sacrifice their traditional autonomy and dedicated to working toward the creation of such norms as a priority objective—something Jimmy Carter seemed willing to do early in his presidency. Similar sacrifices and priorities would have to be volunteered by lesser administration officials, from the Cabinet down to the agencies. Then the rebirth of citizen politics that Thomas Cronin (1975) has advocated would have to occur. Increasing citizen involvement in politics would require not only a continuation of the skeptical watchfulness of the press and other media. It would also be necessary that schools and universities make special efforts to cultivate an increasingly vigilant and militant citizen scrutiny of the presidency, constantly encouraging and renewing the expectation that the president be candid and hold himself accountable. Each generation of children would have to be taught to expect this and to insist upon it—to see it as essential to the health of the republic.

If it were possible to implant such norms deep within the political culture, just as our traditional reverence for the presidency has, until very recently, been imbedded in our culture, then it might be possible to discourage the use of deception as a political resource. Only if such norms and practices took root and flourished could the lure of expedient misrepresentation be significantly reduced. But the influence of intensified scrutiny, plus widely accepted and well-established norms of openness, candor and authenticity, could produce genuine changes in the ways presidents perform their advocacy and symbolic functions. Performance of these functions might no longer encourage presidents to misrepresent themselves, as they now routinely do.

Two problems with relying on this approach must be mentioned. First, it would require a simultaneous solidarity and resolve among all the major sectors of society—government, media, education, and the people—to bring it off. This of course, would be enormously difficult to achieve. Next, and even more difficult, means would have to be found to sustain the vigilant protection of these values across the generations, without need for the stimulus of presidential misbehavior. Intense citizen feelings about any political object are scarce, fleeting, and transitory. Lulls in the people's vigilance are near-inevitable. And such lulls would invite new efforts to deceive. By itself, then, this avenue of reform would likely prove insufficient. Citizen apathy makes total reliance on this reform a poor course of action.

One last potential measure—significant both as a deterrent and as a punishment—deserves brief mention. It is the legislative motion to censure. This could sharply curb presidential lying. Though often dismissed as little more than a slap on the wrist, this measure could upbraid an unruly president. Among other things, it could: (1) galvanize the people into the kind of wary watchfulness needed to sustain truth norms; (2) intensify and give focus to the probes and excavations of the press; (3) lower—or at least threaten—the president's stock with his friends and constituencies, and otherwise add to his store of headaches. Something like this has a chance to be accepted, if only because it seems harmlessly symbolic. Yet it is potentially a powerful disincentive to lying and other forms of presidential misbehavior.

Unsurprisingly, we find no certain cure for presidential lying, though each of the options discussed could supplement others, and the right combination might offer some measure of improvement. These and other reforms suggested by the presidential experience are considered more carefully in the last chapter. For now we must turn to the last of the exposures inherent in the president's job—a pressure whose power to shape presidential behavior is strong, and perhaps more dangerous, than stress, deference, or dissonance. Frustration is the ultimate threat to a president's standing—in his own eyes and in the eyes of history. In the minds of some, it creates the pressure to prevail at any cost.

NOTES

1. Though the research evidence is inconclusive, such research as is available points to (1) a general social disposition of moral restraint, and (2) a widespread social mores which frowns on deceit because it is

socially disruptive (see Wright, 1971, p. 50–78). Individuals vary greatly, but the fear of other people's censure is a powerful motive in most of us. This serves to inhibit lying behavior, particularly when the risk of detection is perceived to be great. Presidents, as beings apart, seem to be tacitly accorded special freedom from these mores by those around them. Presidents enjoy a kind of unusual social credit that frees them, not from scrutiny, but from the kind of morally judgmental scrutiny others attract in face-to-face settings. Moreover, the president has unparalleled resources for minimizing the risk of detection.

2. The "effective constraints" which are internal to the president include any enduring mental predispositions, such as beliefs, attitudes, or values, which construe lying or misrepresentation as morally wrong. Such are the "private sentiments" discussed in the text, which, when they conflict with the subject's behavior, produce cognitive dissonance. For a discussion of the human need for internalized moral guidance, see Rokeach, *The Nature of Human Values* (1973).

3. Some would argue that success at *any* level in American politics extinguishes personal truthtelling norms early on. And certainly many presidents arrive at the White House with their scruples already firmly in check, long accustomed, in Bailey's phrase, to "rowing toward their objectives with muffled oars."

4. I argue that certain kinds of presidential lying, once revealed, threaten the *legitimacy* of the presidency, as defined in Note 6. But American history makes it clear that there is no straightforward relationship between presidential lying and citizen outrage. James K. Polk's cunning orchestration of the Mexican War—aimed at the acquisition of California and Texas—was justly branded as deceitful by much of the contemporary press. Similarly, Theodore Roosevelt's machinations in connection with the acquisition of the Panama Canal Zone were known to be less than straightforward at the time. Yet, unlike Watergate and Vietnam, these presidential deceptions produced no sustained or widespread public outrage. The Mexico–Panama incidents prompt me to offer a speculative hypothesis about citizen response to presidential deceit: When there is some justification for the behavior (e.g., Polk's trumped-up attack on American troops or the Canal's critical importance to American economic interests), when there is something to be gained by it, something perceived as beneficial to the political system as a whole (e.g., Texas, California, and

the Panama Canal), presidential deception will be countenanced. Put another way, the more that is in it for us, the greater the moral departure we can tolerate in our presidents. Unlike Watergate and Vietnam, the victims of the Mexico–Panama deceptions were not Americans but foreigners. But when we, the people, are the objects of the ruse, and if it costs us something (e.g., sons, money, pride), we feel duped, misled, exploited, and outraged.

5. David Easton (1965, p. 279) defines legitimacy as a "conviction on the part of the [citizen] that it is *right* and *proper* for him to accept and obey the authorities and to abide by the requirements of the regime." Both citizens and rulers have a *vested interest* in maintaining a legitimate political order. For citizens, legitimacy is desirable because it sustains political order and stability, and reinforces safe, well-established procedures. From the standpoint of protecting life and property, the first purpose of government, such conditions are greatly preferable to chaos. From the *authorities'* point of view, Easton (1965, p. 249) argues that "the inculcation of a sense of legitimacy is probably the *single most effective device* for regulating the flow of diffuse support [a reservoir of acquiescent good-will] in favor of both the authorities and the regime" [emphasis mine]. Easton (1965, p. 292) contends that the *origins* of legitimacy are three-fold: (1) a sanctifying ideology; (2) a stable political structure (e.g., such organizations and procedures as are described in the U.S. Constitution); and (3) the personal qualities of leaders. The *objects* of legitimacy sentiments, on the other hand, are either the norms and structures of the regime, or the authorities themselves (e.g., the president). Of critical importance to maintaining legitimacy is the correspondence between, on the one hand, the behavior of the authorities, and, on the other, the sanctifying ideology from which their moral authority derives. Easton noted that ". . .especially in those systems displaying a high degree of *stability* the power of the authorities and the regime both depend on *continuing validation* through some set of values, a legitimating ideology." Easton (1965, p. 290) defines an *ideology* as "articulated sets of ideals, ends, and purposes, which help [citizens] to interpret the past, explain the present, and offer a vision for the future. They thus describe the aims for which some members feel political power *ought* to be used, and its limits."

6. Johnson's bitterness toward his critics was always intense, but grew stronger toward the end: "In the immediate hours after his announce-

ment [that he would not seek re-election] he bitterly denounced his worst critics. He flailed the press, once again heaping most of the blame for his credibility problems on reporters and broadcasters. He showed equal scorn for his Senate adversaries, such as Fulbright. Of course, Bobby Kennedy was castigated" (Sidey, 1968:281).

7. The signs of damaged legitimacy were plentiful. Three times in 1967, the Gallup pollsters asked: "Do you think the Johnson Administration is or is not telling the public all it should know about the Vietnam War?" Only twenty-one to twenty-four percent thought it was, while sixty-five to seventy percent thought it wasn't (Gallup Opinion Index cited in Mueller, 1973, p. 113). Further, there was widespread resistance to military conscription; vitriolic caricature and criticism of Johnson was rampant; the liberal (democratic and intellectual) community had totally rejected the war and Johnson's moral right to wage it; the peace movement was visible, vocal, and increasingly active (marches and demonstrations); and Johnson found it impossible to make appearances or deliver public addresses except on military bases: In sum, the ethical force of, and moral support for, his administration had evaporated.

8. The following were among the ideological transgressions of the war effort: (1) the absence of a plausible *legal* justification; (2) indiscriminate destruction of the life and property of noncombatant Vietnamese citizens; (3) military interference in the internal affairs of a sovereign state, and (4) the absence of a clear and widely acceptable *moral* rationale (the rationale of containing communism had lost its force).

9. My value judgment. The signs of a weak bond include widespread cynicism toward new revelations of past presidential transgressions: to wit, the "ho-hum" public reaction to the allegations of Bill Moyers and CBS News that John and Robert Kennedy may have enlisted the aid of the Mafia, and did engage the CIA, in efforts to assassinate Cuban Premier Fidel Castro. Such accusations would have been astounding and breathtaking as recently as the mid-1960s. Another sign is that the people are hungry for a restoration of moral integrity, as is suggested by the enthusiastic public support for President Carter's somewhat clumsy (by diplomatic standards) efforts, spearheaded by U.N. Ambassador Andrew Young, to restore the tattered virtue of the United States on the international stage.

10. As Derek Wright observes in *The Psychology of Moral Behavior* (1971, p. 50), temptation situations have come to be accepted as *the*

tests of moral strength: "As with all tests, some people pass, others fail, *though all are presumed to fail sometimes*" [emphasis mine].

11. *Time* Magazine (August 8, 1977, p. 8) argued in a cover story:

All this activity and rhetoric has had a significant effect at home. After the guilt-ridden defeat in Vietnam and the shocks of Watergate, Carter has given many Americans a renewed feeling that they are standing for something good in the world. He has done this in his own special style, but in the tradition of Wilson, Roosevelt and Dulles, who, in very different ways, affirmed that U.S. foreign policy must have a moral content. And in a televised interview with ABC news, Carter claimed credit for restoring the people's confidence in government ("The Carter Report Card," ABC News Broadcast, August 14, 1977). However durable this accomplishment proves to be, Carter's behavior during his first six months in office revealed a shrewd appreciation for the moral basis of legitimacy.

Those who would carry on great public schemes must be-proof against the worst fatiguing delays, the most mortifying disappointments, the most shocking insults, and worst of all, the presumptuous judgment of the ignorant upon their designs.

EDMUND BURKE, quoted in STEINBERG, *Sam Johnson's Boy*

By this time it is clear that presidents are buffeted by forceful stimulation of various kinds, stimulation which originates outside the president's skull in the network of exposures and circumstances that structure his job. I have acknowledged repeatedly that individual presidents differ in their responses to this common stimulation, but I have argued that the average press and intensity of the exposures, the routine force of the influences that work upon presidents, is sufficient to have some impact on the attitudes and behavior of any human being, regardless of the strength, nature, or quality of his character. Furthermore, I have implied that the directional flow of this influence is by and large undesirable, when measured against the values of political stability, democracy, and rational performance effectiveness criteria. Stress consumes the president's energy

FRUSTRATION:
The Pressure
To Prevail

6

and encourages him to isolate himself from the currents of opinion outside the White House, all of which obviously compromises his ability to perform effectively. Deference distorts a president's ability to perceive and test reality, accentuates his isolation, and emboldens him to act on the basis of misinformed decisional premises. The presidency encourages presidents to lie; and dissonance, the psychological state which follows upon situational surrender to temptation, motivates an erosion of the president's personal scruples against lying, and can lead him to delude himself about his own veracity. And in some circumstances, I have argued, presidential deception can undermine the legitimacy and the stability of the national political order.

The behavioral consequences of frustration, the pressure to prevail, are no less threatening to the values identified to and particularly to democratic values. The last of the influence vectors to be considered, frustration is, if anything, more direct and more forceful as a motivator of dangerous presidential behavior than the other pressures. I address these and other issues in the present chapter. But the inevitability of frustration as a presidential experience is the first point that must be established.

ORIGIN: THE POLICY ADVOCATE FUNCTION

The United States Constitution vests the policy-making powers primarily with the Congress. Yet historical exigencies, coupled with Constitutional clauses traditionally interpreted as justifying presidential involvement in policy advocacy, led Congress to yield the initiative in this area to the president. As the institution best positioned, by dint of internal unity and the open-endedness of its constitutional mandate, to cope with the unexpected, the executive has had the greater historical responsibility for developing and advocating solutions to emergent national problems.

But yielding the initiative has not proved equivalent to surrendering its policy-making powers. Congress must approve of any presidential initiative that involves legislation, and it has been jealous of this prerogative. Congress also has the formal power to supervise and chastise the executive branch, and the stormy history of the relations between the president and Congress is testimony to the latter's sustained willingness to use its power (Binkley, 1962). Thus, the Congress is, and nearly always has been, a major constraint on the president's discretion. But it is by no means the only constraint. As Rexford Tugwell (1960, p. 31) observes:

> [The president] was made independent of, in many ways opposed to, and yet inescapably coordinate with, the other Branches; and that, in creating him, the framers established a state of tension and uncertainty which would be unremitting.

The other branch is, of course, the Supreme Court, which has intermittently but successfully thwarted presidential initiatives since the Jefferson era. To the Congress and the Supreme Court must be added a bewildering variety of other formal and informal power centers. The press, mentioned earlier in connection with presidential stress, plays a critical substantive role in reviewing the plans of presidents, and does much to coalesce and solidify public opposition to the president's initiatives. And several powerful governmental and extra-governmental bodies—bureaucracies, regulatory agencies, and interest groups too numerous to mention here—complete the set of potential obstacles to presidential initiatives. These forces comprise the external sources of frustration, which psychologists define as an obstruction in the path between an organism and its objective (Costello and Zalkind, 1963).

Set against these obstacles is the view—rooted in the traditions of the presidency and the expectations of the people—that a president worth his salt finds ways to prevail over opposition and to put his personal stamp on policy outcomes. Americans have been historically leery of political power, yet they cannot help but admire and support presidential power. One of the very few empirical studies of adult attitudes toward the presidency (Sigel, 1969) strongly confirmed the following three hypotheses:

1. Voters want strong presidents who know how to lead and how to make their will prevail.

2. Because Americans are afraid of political power, and precisely because they have accorded the president so much of it, they also wish to curb his power lest he abuse it.
3. Voters prefer traits in a president which are characteristic of power rather than homey human traits of virtues.

One can speculate whether, given the abuses of presidential power in recent years, the results of this dated study would hold true as this is written. I would expect that apart from increasingly strong support for the second hypothesis, a vigorous advocacy presidency, purged of the moral transgressions of Watergate and Vietnam, would still enjoy widespread support. Certainly Jimmy Carter, whose presidential behavior in his first six months was favorably received by the public, conducted himself in the advocacy style of the strong, "Jeffersonian" presidents. And there has been no discernible movement away from the traditions of the presidency, embedded in the judgments of historians, which ennoble and reward presidential success and dominance. Hapless presidents who lose control of events or allow themselves to be outmaneuvered (e.g., Grant, Harding, Buchanan) can expect to be relegated to the "below average" or "failure" categories. A president who aspires to greatness in the eyes of history, then, is still likely to identify with "aggressive" models of the presidency, such as are embodied in Corwin's discussion of the "strong" (versus "weak") presidency, Burns's "Hamiltonian" or "Jeffersonian" models, Theodore Roosevelt's "Stewardship" theory, or FDR's "expansionist" presidency. Despite recent setbacks, the trans-historical faith in presidential power as, in some respects, a good unto itself, is alive and well.[1] The norms of the presidency, the president's policy advocate responsibilities, the judgments of historians, and the expectations of the people: All stand as inducements for any president to find a way to work his will.

Given these inducements, it is near-certain that any president will aspire to leave some record of policy achievement. But given the existence of other power centers capable of thwarting him, it is equally certain that he will be thwarted—in small and large ways—throughout his tenure. Presidential policy initiatives attract controversy like a magnet. It is inevitable, then, that presidents will be exposed to external frustration in the form of legitimate political opposition. The greater a president's policy ambitions, the greater will be his exposure to such opposition.

PSYCHOLOGICAL MEANING

Internally, a president's feeling of frustration stems from the discrepancy between what he hopes to accomplish and what he is able to attain after the necessary accomodation of legitimate political opposition. It is the fate of most American presidents to fall short of their important objectives. Indeed, settling for "half a loaf" is the classic experience of democratic political leadership. John Quincy Adams's dreams of internal improvements, Harry Truman's civil rights ambitions, Wilson's hope for a League of Nations led by the United States, and John Kennedy's New Frontier are but a few of the dashed presidential hopes that could be cited. Most presidents find barriers thrown up to derail even the most innocuous and well-intentioned initiatives—to the point where opposition comes to seem not principled and reasoned but mindless and instinctive—in the spirit of Edmund Burke's warning that opened this chapter. The path to policy consensus is so studded with intransigent land mines that many a president must have shared Richard Nixon's fear of seeming a "pitiful, helpless giant," unable for all his vaunted power to put the Lilliputians to rout.

To appreciate the private significance of presidential frustration, we must bear in mind that, unlike stress, frustration describes those instances where the president enters the political arena with a goal he wants to attain, stakes his prestige on the outcome, and then finds himself thwarted by legitimate political opposition. The distinction between stress and frustration thus rests with presidential initiative. Both pressures may activate the feeling of responsibility. Both may embody a commitment of self in circumstances that carry a high risk of failure for the president. But the pain of failure, and the motivation to avoid it, can be presumed to be greater in the case of frustration—if only because of the greater personal investment implied by the unambiguous advocacy posture. Franklin D. Roosevelt, who didn't "expect a hit every time I come to bat," was nonetheless moved, by the threat of watching his New Deal legislation set aside by the high court, to try to reconstitute that body in order to protect his achievement. And Woodrow Wilson, who was capable of expedient compromise on issues of relative indifference to him, became unyielding and adamant when opposed on matters like the League of Nations, in which he had invested his self-esteem. Even George Washington, among the most temperate of presidents, occasionally reacted to frustration with intransigent stubbornness. Washington went before the Senate to seek "advice and consent" to a treaty he had arranged with the Creek Indians. He was so incensed by the stubborn opposition he encountered there that he vowed he would "be damned if [he] ever went there again," thus setting a precedent that remained undisturbed until Gerald Ford presented himself to explain his decision to pardon Richard Nixon (Flexner, 1970).

Frustration is psychologically meaningful, then, because it forces the president to confront evidence of his own impotence in areas likely to concern him deeply and personally—issues on which he has chosen to stake his prestige and his claim to a place in history. If success builds self-esteem, frustration—the threat of failure—can damage it. Failure also damages the president's public standing and professional reputation. It thus feeds on itself. The threat of failure can be expected to motivate intense, and in some cases desperate, presidential efforts to circumvent and override the opposition.

CUMULATIVE PSYCHOLOGICAL IMPACTS

A Kennedy aide (quoted in Cronin, 1975, p. 153) said:

> Everybody believes in democracy until he gets to the White House and then you begin to believe in dictatorship because it's so hard to get things done. Everytime you turn around, people resist you.

I have argued that there is a fundamental inconsistency between the constraints imposed on the executive by the Constitution and the expectations we have for presidential boldness, vigor, and dominance. Presidents are hamstrung by design, yet for the most part, the revered presidents have been those who bent their chains beyond recognition. The successful presidents are those who, despite all constraints, find ways to shape events and put their personal stamp on outcomes. Widespread external expectations tend to encourage and reinforce aggressive reactions to frustration.

But not all recent presidents have responded to these expectations. Dwight Eisenhower, for example, simply refused to be baited into aggressive responses to challenges to his leadership. His presidential self-concept was, in James McGregor Burns's language, "Madisonian." So far as we can tell, he genuinely respected the limits imposed on the president by shared executive legislative powers. [2]

The responders have been Hamiltonians, updated to include identification with the modern paradigm for assertive presidents, Franklin D. Roosevelt. For these presidents, self-respect requires vigorous response to challenge and sustained efforts at political dominance. They have been in the majority since FDR. And in the search for dominance, it is they who have found the president's limited constitutional powers and his informal powers of persuasion to be an impotent store of options and resources with which to shape events. Pitched and well-publicized battle—often resulting in new definitions of presidential power—has been the historically preferred response for successful presidents. Rogow and Lasswell (1963) note that the presidents who left their mark on history have been those whose relations with the other branches were infrequently harmonious and cordial.

This raises another question, involving the distinction between frustration, on the one hand, and the temptation to deceive, described in the previous chapter, on the other. Why open conflict, and not deception, as a stratagem for coping with opposition?

My answer is that while deception of various sorts may well be employed in response to challenges to presidential leadership (e.g., withholding information that could aid and abet the opposition), a defining characteristic of frustration is its very "publicness." That is, frustration, in the context of the presidency, by definition involves a widely observed and clearly understood challenge to the president's stature and standing. The circumstances that tempt a president to lie in order to achieve his goals are, on the other hand, murkier, and less clear-cut. In such instances as Lyndon Johnson's trade-off between Vietnam and the Great Society, others do not yet perceive the conflicts that have crystallized in the president's mind, and which tempt him to deceive. The very ambiguity of the situation in the minds of others is what makes deception seem a plausible course of action.

But because with frustration the challenge is public, the president's response—or at least the evidence of his final triumph—and his role in bringing it about, must also be public if it is to vindicate his standing in the eyes of others. Evasive means of coping with open defiance of the president would be tantamount to public acknowledgment that the president has lost the struggle and been driven underground. To a president faced with open defiance of his leadership, it will frequently seem that the only viable alternative to capitulation is to join the battle with his antagonist in the full view of those he seeks to lead.

It is apparent that every presidential initiative, from the most trivial to the most consequential, will galvanize some opposition. Presidents are aware of this, expect it, and, to some extent, are prepared for it. But as human beings, we can expect them to feel some twinge of irritation—some internal feelings of frustration—at each such encounter. It is clear that opposition to his major aspirations will have the greatest psychological impact and the greatest motivational power. But once again, the relevant question is prompted by the psychological truism that a recurring stimulus eventually produces a conditioned response. As his encounters with large and small obstacles accumulate in the course of his term, what can we expect that the long-term psychological consequences—the socialization effect—will be? How does recurring exposure to trivial and consequential frustrations influence the enduring attitudes, orientations, dispositions—the mental states—of presidents in general?

Table 4   Patterns of Presidential Frustration

ROLE DEMAND	INEVITABLE EXPOSURE	PSYCHOLOGICAL MEANING
Policy advocate	Determined opposition to policy initiatives	Possibility of failure
		Threat to self-concept
PSYCHOLOGICAL EXPERIENCE	CUMULATIVE PSYCHOLOGICAL IMPACT[a]	PRESIDENTIAL BEHAVIOR[a]
Frustration	Erosion of respect for "traditional" democratic norms	Arrogation of power (e.g., impoundment of funds, misuse of the CIA and the FBI
	Increased preoccupation with personal success and survival, and with prevailing over opposition despite its legitimacy	Plebiscitary presidency (e.g., strategy of discrediting discrediting press and Congress; accountable only to voters)
		Provocation of conflict (e.g., Wilson and League of Nations dispute, FDR's Supreme Court "packing" scheme)

[a]varies with individual differences.

Table 4 encapsules the answers offered here, and summarizes the patterns of frustration described in this chapter. It is likely that exposure to frustration will result in increased preoccupation with personal success and survival, relative to other perhaps more important values that might be imbedded in a contest of wills. And as the president searches for ways to prevail over opposition, it is likely, apropos of the feelings expressed by the Kennedy aide in the quote that began this section, that there will occur a gradual and subtle erosion of respect for such "traditional" democratic norms as strict adherence to constitutional processes, and for the legitimacy of countervailing political institutions.

BEHAVIORAL OUTCOMES

The observable signs of these emergent feeling states—the presidential behaviors that point to their existence—include numerous acts of presidential defiance and aggression that range from outright usurpation of power to rigid and obdurate insistence on prevailing at any cost. Because frustration threatens the president's standing in his own and others' eyes, it has often provoked him to overstep his bounds, secure in the knowledge that such behavior has frequently been sanctioned by glory in the past. The collection of excesses that Arthur Schlesinger (1973) has variously termed the "imperial" or "plebiscitary" presidency is the most extreme and systematic reaction thus far. It involves a strategy of discrediting the opposition— notably the press and the Congress—for the benefit of the public. This forces the opposition into a defensive posture, which frees the president to proceed at will, accountable *only* to the electorate, and then only once in four years.

Other, less comprehensive arrogations of power, such as the impoundment of funds as a means of circumventing the Congressional power of the purse in order to impose the president's financial priorities, or the use of federal police agencies like the FBI or the CIA to obtain information for use in discrediting the opposition, can also be attributed to frustration, as can the use of official administration spokesmen who use verbal aggression to mobilize public opinion against the president's opponents. Also, the oft-noted "retreat" into foreign affairs can be seen as at least a partial consequence of presidential frustration on the domestic front. Here, the president in effect throws up his hands at home, but asserts himself boldly in international affairs. Though he may strain the constitutional checks on his foreign actions, he does so in the context of a tradition of presidential dominance that has not been successfully challenged.

But perhaps the most damaging and self-defeating presidential response to frustration involves engagement in open conflict with one or both of the two major branches of government. There have been two major instances of this in the present century. Woodrow Wilson's petulant and self-indulgent insistence that the Senate ratify the

League of Nations proposal in precisely the form that he, Wilson, had proffered it, had the effect of delaying U.S. participation in the organized world community until after World War II. And in the short run, the conflict with the Senate served to destroy Wilson's effectiveness as president. Similarly, Franklin D. Roosevelt's irritation at the Supreme Court's treatment of his cherished New Deal legislation prompted him to try to alter that body in order to guarantee smooth passage for his personal priorities. So confident was Roosevelt that his vision was the true one that he was willing to change the face of the government in order to work his will.

ROOSEVELT VS. THE SUPREME COURT

To the vast majority of his contemporaries, Franklin D. Roosevelt's legislative ambitions and successes spelled the difference between privation and prosperity. During his first term in office, and particularly during the fabled "100 days," he had engineered a series of legislative measures through Congress which had reversed the depression and established a new philosophy of government which held it desirable and appropriate for government to provide citizens with a measure of protection from the hazards of economic ruin. A multitude of "alphabet" agencies and programs was established to deal with specific needs—the Emergency Banking Relief Act, the Federal Emergency Relief Act, the Tennessee Valley Authority Act, the Emergency Farm Mortgage Act, the National Industrial Recovery Act, the Civil Works Administration (CWA), the Civilian Conservation Corps (CCC)—the list goes on and on. The impact of these measures on the country's well-being—and on Roosevelt's popularity—was dramatic. Prosperity and national self-confidence increased. And Roosevelt, re-elected in 1936 by the greatest margin in history, had a personal triumph without precedent in presidential politics.

But just more than a year before this staggering triumph, on May 27, 1935, the Supreme Court had voted nine to zero to declare the National Industrial Recovery Act (NIRA) unconstitutional, arguing that the Federal Government's regulation of business was an illegal intervention in intrastate affairs. Based as it was on a narrow interpretation of the interstate commerce clause of the Constitution, this decision augured poorly for much of the rest of the New Deal, which clearly depended for its survival upon a less restrictive interpretation of that clause. And, as expected, the Court struck down other vital legislation: The Railroad Pension Act and the Guffey-Snyder Coal Act were among the victims. In all, nine decisions unfavorable to the New Deal were handed down. It seemed as if the legislative revolution of the New Deal was doomed to extinction.

Roosevelt was furious. But with the 1936 election approaching, he was certain of a large vote of public confidence. So he bided his time, coping as best he could with the adverse consequences of the Court's decisions. Once re-elected, however, he allowed his irritation to surface. In his address to a joint session of Congress on January 6, 1937, (quoted in Corwin, 1957, p. 290) he said:

> Means must be found to adapt our legal forms and our judicial interpretations to the actual present national needs of the largest progressive democracy in the modern world.

The tone was relatively moderate. But as later events would prove, his tone belied more aggressive intentions. His state of mind at the time is suggested by Corwin (1957, p. 290), who writes:

> The huge popular endorsement that this [the 1936 election] gave Mr. Roosevelt he not unreasonably interpreted as a mandate to establish certain legislation that by theories then dominant on the Court was clearly unconstitutional. The President was thus confronted with a difficult problem of political leadership: Was he to postpone his program indefinitely while his political following dissolved, or was he to remove the principal obstacle to success within a comparatively brief time?

We know that he had absolutely no intention, then or later, of passively accepting the judgment of the Court. He was, in fact, aflame with righteous indignation at the "nine old men" who presumed to defy the will of the people, and, it can be argued, his own will.

There is no disputing the fact that the Court's intransigent posture was in conflict with the popular will. But one can fairly dispute any claim that Roosevelt's plans and acts were motivated solely by a selfless desire to express the will of the people. These were his programs and it was his success that the Court was threatening. The massive popular support that he enjoyed lent force to his anger. But it should not be allowed to obscure the fact that Roosevelt was ego-involved. At least in part, he was motivated by the desire to continue the unchecked personal dominance he had exercised over the course of government for the previous four years.

But, as political figures are wont to do, Roosevelt (quoted in American Heritage History, 1968, p. 805) publicly framed the conflict, not in the personal terms that he felt it, but in terms of popular sovereignty:

> [The issue is] whether the kind of government which the people had voted for in 1932, 1934, and 1936 was to be permitted by the Supreme Court to function, and whether the Court, functioning as a super legislature, could torture the Constitution to conform to its outmoded economic beliefs.

The fact is that Roosevelt was frustrated, and he was to respond with aggression. That his response was fueled by the emotions that tend to accompany frustration—anger, defiance, grim determination—is attested to by the wholly uncharacteristic sloppiness and lack of adroitness with which he moved to work his will. Emboldened by his electoral mandate and irritated at the temerity of the Court, he acted unilaterally, expecting to put the Court in its place once and for all (Tugwell, 1960, p. 426):

> The President was very evidently intent on a showdown: He had not forgiven the challenge to his leadership represented by the invalidations of the years just past. He meant to make it impossible in future for the Court to reject measures agreed on by the President and the Congress.

Without even consulting the democratic party leaders on the Hill, he introduced his Judicial Reform Bill. Even in anger, however, his longstanding penchant for guile led him to couch his proposal in unstraightforward terms. Instead of seeking legislative remedies for the specific problem at hand—the judicial excesses of the Court—Roosevelt aimed his reform proposal at a separate and largely unrelated issue: the contrivance of judicial old age. His plan would have given him the right to appoint one new justice (up to a total of fifteen) for each justice who refused to retire six months after reaching the age of seventy.

With the conflict between the president and the Court widely known, and with its true nature clearly understood by any informed observer, why did Roosevelt try to obscure his plainly transparent effort to unseat those Supreme Court Justices who had ruled against the New Deal by trumping up the old age issue? We can speculate that his political intuition told him that his prospects for success would be greater if he did not appear to be challenging the Court's unquestioned right to rule on the substance of legislation. But whatever led him to this course, it proved to be a serious miscalculation. First, by confusing the issue, it dissipated the moral force behind the claim that the Court was obstructing positive governmental action to meet pressing national needs. No one was fooled by his indirection. Rather, people were struck by its deviousness, and angered that he would compromise his own legitimacy with such a transparent and irrelevant ploy. His stratagem played right into the hands of his conservative opponents, who were able to shift attention from the focal issue to the question of Roosevelt's craftiness.

Next, even as the court-packing measure was under discussion within the Senate Judiciary Committee, his own party congressmen began to repudiate him. Before long, an important segment of the Congress had aligned itself with the Court. Soon the conflict seemed to pit the president alone against the other branches. Press reaction was almost unanimously unfavorable. And the voters who had just given Roosevelt his own record mandate wavered in their support. Said one elderly lady (quoted in Corwin, 1957, p. 483):

The founders of our country knew what they were doing when they provided for nine judges. If nine were good enough for President Washington, they should be good enough for President Roosevelt. I don't see why he needs fifteen.

The method he had chosen became more of a cause célèbre than the substance of his criticism of the Court (Hargrove, 1966). For Roosevelt had seriously miscalculated the strength of the Court's symbolic stature (Finer, 1960, p. 137):

A President can be too clever. Roosevelt overreached himself in attempting to reform the Supreme Court. Surely this was, and is, so hallowed an American institution that nothing less than open and frank action (if anything at all) would have succeeded? A surreptitious course brought suspicion of his purpose and increased distrust of the man.

The dénouement was that the most astute politician ever to occupy the White House suffered his first major political defeat in the course of the first serious struggle between the three branches since the days of reconstruction (Tugwell, 1960). As Robert Sherwood (1948, p. 169) observes:

It is true that he burned his fingers badly on the Supreme Court packing issue when, following his smashing victory in the 1936 election, he suffered from an excess of overconfidence, and his exasperation resulting from defeat on this issue led him to burn his fingers again in the attempted purge [of democratic congressmen who had opposed his reform measure].

Even though it is obvious that the Court was exceeding its own informal bounds, and thus shared responsibility for this threat to its historic status, we must still conclude that Roosevelt's attack constituted a serious threat, both to the stability of the Court, and to the democratic values that underlie its exalted position in the institutional trilogy. The questions we must ask are: How could such an accomplished student of politics, a brilliantly successful active-positive president, have miscalculated so badly? And why was he willing to risk the destruction, or at least the diminution, of an historically invaluable institution, just so that he might continue unchecked his personal direction of governmental affairs? Why wasn't it apparent to Roosevelt that the forces of change that he represented were greater than himself, and would have prevailed just as readily, in spite of his actions, as they did in fact?

The answer, I think, is that Roosevelt wanted the credit for disciplining the Court. For all of his storied adroitness, he was still no more and no less than a solitary human being, excited and emboldened by his astounding success and massive public support, into the emotional conviction that his will was destined to prevail. So firm was this conviction that when he was externally and internally frustrated, his emotional state compromised his judgment. His determination to win was, under the circumstances, the highest operative value. He showed himself quite willing to risk any adverse, long-term consequences for stability or democracy in order to maintain his personal centrality. Only his blatant lack of respect for the legitimacy of the Court kept him from succeeding. Had he fully exercised the political skill for which he is famous, he might have avoided the outrage that turned the tide of public opinion against him and succeeded in permanently weakening the Supreme Court.

My point in offering this interpretation of one of the best of our presidents is that this is really the most we can expect from human beings, caught up in their passions, who single-handedly wield the executive power of government. Neither skill, wisdom, nor strength of character is sufficient to stay or discipline the combination of power and righteous anger.

WHAT CAN BE DONE?

Those presidential actions and behaviors plausibly attributed to frustration cover the spectrum of domestic and foreign executive responsibilities. Presidents have arrogated power in both realms since the earliest days of the republic, often in response to challenges to their leadership. Indeed, it can be argued that frustration has been an important impetus for the intermittent but cumulative expansion of presidential power—from its initial co-equality with the other branches to its present position of de facto supremacy. Because of the abiding strain of fear and mistrust of executive power in the national psyche, means have been contrived for "bringing the president to heel" when he oversteps his bounds. These means are the traditional solutions to the problems of executive aggression and usurpation—solutions which, when seen in the light of the seemingly unstoppable growth in presidential power, seem less than adequate.

Presidents have been and can be stopped by the Court. Jefferson, FDR, Truman, and Nixon are among the presidents who could bear witness to this. But the Court has been conservative—reluctant to give the president direct orders, to involve itself in topical political matters, or to issue broadly applicable directives. The "switch in time that saved nine"—the Court's self-directed retreat from its opposition to the New Deal legislation—bespeaks its sensitivity to the currents of public opinion, and its appreciation for the fragility of its own moral claim to the obedience of presidents and citizens alike (McCloskey, 1960).

Presidents have been and can be stopped by the Congress. Following upon the Johnson and Nixon presidencies, with their domestic and foreign policy excesses, the Congress reasserted itself, enacting such legislation as the War Powers Act of 1973, which limits the president's right to wage war without approval (Koenig, 1975, pp. 219–220). Additional legislation, affecting the president's liberties with appropriated funds, requires that he supply lists of impounded funds every thirty days, and provides that if an impoundment is not approved by Congress within sixty days, the funds must be spent (Lammers, 1976, p. 215). The effectiveness of this legislation was untested when this was written, but it represented significant new constraints on presidential discretion. And if all else fails, there is always the "blunt instrument" of impeachment proceedings.

Presidents have been and can be stopped by the press. Historic revelations of corruption and graft, television coverage of the Vietnam war, and investigative reporting such as that of Woodward and Bernstein (1976) have all played major roles in the disciplining of presidents.

And most importantly, presidents have been and can be stopped by the people—via elections and groundswell rejections. Presidents anticipate public reactions to their plans, and this can serve as a before the fact constraint (e.g., "Will it play in Peoria?"). More effective, unfortunately, are ex post facto public reactions, some of which, like that to Nixon's firing of Cox, are strong enough to drive the man from office.

These four major constraints have functioned with some effectiveness. Each has served at one time or another to arrest presidential abuses. As things stand, with a unitary executive who must possess broad discretionary powers in order to perform effectively the functions that he is assigned by custom and the Constitution, it would be unwise to advocate the creation of additional, comparably powerful checks. More checks would hamstring the executive agency to the point where the generic functions would have to be performed by other bodies.

But more important, it should be remembered that the obstacles and constraints just described—the Court, the Congress, the press, and the people—are the sources of presidential frustration. These are the barriers which, in time, can erode the president's valuation of democratic and constitutional processes. These are the constraints which, given the trans-historical celebration of presidential potency, a president comes to view as mere tests of his mettle—an obstacle course he must run and circumvent in order to win the prize of historical respect.

There is an invidious psychological dynamic at work here. Formal and informal constraints established to preserve and protect democratic processes, and intended as symbols of democratic values, worthy of respect in their own right, instead get perceived by too many presidents as threats to their personal status, enemies to be vanquished, opponents to be outmaneuvered in the struggle for self-validation and historical vindication. The more stubborn and implacable the opposition, the greater the feeling of potency when it is overcome. The incentive system of the contemporary presidency is capable of reducing constitutional processes to a self-defeating war game, whose ultimate victims are the values and the stability of the political system.

Thus the root problem, far from being solved by the existing constraints on presidential discretion, is instead exacerbated by those constraints. They can stop presidents, but, in the spirit of challenging games, as often as not they serve only to incite them to greater boldness and creativity in the search for dominance.

If the past is the surest available predictor of the future, we can expect the unrelieved tension between the president and his constitutional adversaries to continue; to erupt periodically into open conflict; and to result in short-term abridgments of executive power, but in the long run to result in its continued accumulation. Adding more constraints won't help. Somehow, ways must be found either to reduce presidential exposure to frustration, or to restructure the incentives so as to discourage aggressive responses to opposition when it is encountered.

WHOM WE ELECT AND WHAT WE EXPECT

The solutions most likely to be immediately effective are also the solutions that are least practical, least realistic, and least likely of adoption. If, for example, the advocacy function were removed from the presidency and put back in the Congress, if future presidents were not obliged to worry about building support for their policy priorities, they would rarely be exposed to frustration. Or if we took the advice of the long line of scholars and statesmen—stretching from Edmund Randolph at the Constitutional Convention to Herman Finer in the early 1960s—and adopted a group presidency, the resulting depersonalization of the office would probably reduce executive aggression and intra-governmental conflict. But these things, like other far-reaching reforms, are very unlikely to be

adopted without the stimulus of sudden disaster or of other moment-
ous, unforseeable changes.

If we can't simply remove frustration or rebuild the office, what
can be done? One possibility is to try to identify and elect the kinds
of people James David Barber calls the *passive* presidents—those
whose first impulse is to ignore, avoid, or withdraw from frustration
rather than to retaliate against it. Such avoidance tendencies need
not be a sign of weakness or of political impotence in a president.
Nor must they necessarily result in directionless drift, as Barber
himself fears. Dwight Eisenhower—a passive-negative who em-
braced a Madisonian view of the presidency—managed to sustain
the greatest measure of popular approval any president has ever enjoyed, despite a rather low level of policy aspiration. Unlike presidents who identify with vigorous, activist models of the job,
Eisenhower's self-respect was not contingent upon his legislative
box score, or upon his ability to outmaneuver political opponents.
He simply refused to interpret opposition in angry or personal terms,
something that was especially apparent during the McCarthy era.
His "above the battle" stance, while contributing to his impressive
store of public approval, simultaneously enraged the activist liberal
community, who looked upon him as a "do-nothing" president. But
Eisenhower seemed oblivious to their dissatisfaction, apparently
confident that his own interpretation of the responsibilities of the
presidency would stand the test of time. And indeed, the judgments
of his administration offered by political scientists and journalists
have already begun to improve. Neustadt's negative evaluation of
his competence in *Presidential Power* (1960) has been persuasively
answered by Garry Wills's interpretation in his book, *Nixon
Agonistes* (1969). Responding to the charge that Ike was a "do-
nothing" president, Wills opines (p. 130):

> [Eisenhower's critics] fail to appreciate that the conservation of
> authority—or, rather, the reconstitution of it—deserved the high
> priority Eisenhower gave it. He took over a nation full of internal
> doubt and suspicion, summarized in the phrase "the McCarthy Era."
> So successfully did Ike quiet this divisive ferment that his critics
> would, by the end of his time in office, reproach him for running

such a quiet ship. It was a substantial achievement, though not a flashy one. In his customary manner, Ike got the job done, without trumpets. In his foreign policy, he inherited the Cold War and brought a degree of stability and—once again—placidity to the handling of conflicts. He took over a nation at war, a people fearful of atomic holocaust and poisoned milk. He left office to a man who cried for more missiles and for shock troops to fight guerrilla wars by helicopter.

Of course, those who look to an aggressive, activist presidency as essential to national well-being—those who see determined advocacy of substantive solutions to pressing problems as having greater urgency than protection of longer run democracy or system stability values—will view the election of Eisenhower-like characters who place mediation above exhortation as unacceptable. Presumably, they fear the potentially harmful consequences of policy drift more than they do the potentially harmful consequences of frustrating an aggressive president. Certainly there are historical moments when presidential assertiveness and dominance are greatly to be desired. But danger lies, I think, in the routinization of expectations and other incentives that serve to encourage presidential aggression. Dominance as a value unto itself—dominance for the sake of dominance—is encouraged by the evaluative criteria now applied to presidents (Bailey, 1966). It is safer and more prudent to stack the deck against such behavior. Electing passive, or simply temperate people—those displaying little interest in the glories of power—is one way to help stack the deck. Another way would be to push for a redefinition of what constitutes "greatness" in a president. High marks might usefully go to those who "fit" their times in a way that served, or simply did not harm, long-term national values, rather than solely to those who made a towering impact. By such revised standards, Gerald Ford, Grover Cleveland, and James Monroe would rank much higher than they do, while presidents like Jackson or Theodore Roosevelt—men who gloried in the exercise of dominance for its own sake—much lower. Making bad things not happen ought to be just as important as making good things happen.

Barber and others who would rely on character as a solution see a way for us to "have our cake and eat it too." By electing active-positive presidents, we can simultaneously obtain the values of vigorous advocacy plus presidential moderation. Barber argues that this kind of person combines a results-oriented, take-charge dynamism with genuine moral-democratic values of restraint and respect for constitutional processes. The active-positive will push for results, but can be expected to stop short of the dangerous rigidifications displayed by Wilson, Hoover, Johnson, and Nixon. These claims, and other issues involved in evaluating presidential character, are the subjects of Chapter 7.

TRANSITION

This chapter concludes my analysis of the pressures of the presidency. Taken together, the chapters on the pressures have tried to make the point that any president, regardless of the strength or quality of his character, is likely to be influenced in enduring and important ways by the recurring exposures he will inevitably encounter as he goes about his business. And I have argued that the likely consequences of such influence are, on the whole, more than acceptably dangerous to the values of political stability, democracy, and effective presidential performance.

The final portion of this book—a chapter on character and one on reform—assays the two major classes of remedies for the problems posed by the presidential experience. These are often cast as "either/or" alternatives. We can either continue to trust character—renewing our search for the Philosopher-King (or Barber's updated version, the active-positive). Or we can identify structural, procedural, and other changes capable of arresting or diluting the dynamics of influence that have been described.

Americans have always preferred the first alternative. They have never shown themselves willing to entertain major changes in the presidency. They have always considered a change in personnel as the quickest, surest, and easiest solution to presidential abuse or incompetence. Americans have displayed an abiding faith in presidential character—if we can only find the right man or woman for the job, the problems will abate.

Yet my analysis suggests that this faith is misplaced, that character alone is not enough. At best, sterling character is necessary but not sufficient as an antidote to the presidential experience. Of course it makes a difference who is president. But as I argue in Chapter 7, character alone can offer no secure solution to the problems posed by the presidential experience. Important as it is, by itself it is simply not enough.

If we are to avoid further trouble—future Vietnams or Watergates—we must supplement our search for quality presidents with those reforms capable of arresting or lessening the negative influences of the presidential experience. We must either overcome our historic reluctance to tamper with the presidency or resign ourselves to presidential behavior that threatens to harm us as much as it helps us. What we know of the response propensities of humans in general to pressures like those embedded in the presidency makes this a strong probability—one that cannot be dismissed out of hand.

NOTES

1. This faith in presidential power as a good unto itself finds its clearest expression in Richard Neustadt's classic study of *Presidential Power* 1976). In the Preface to the original edition, Neustadt (p. 117) asserts that "the purpose here is to explore the power problem of the man inside the White House. This is the classic problem of the man on top in any political system: How to be on top in fact as well as name." In a critique which underscores the moral neutrality of the book, Professor Richard Loss (1976, p. 75) argues: "The book implicitly assumes among potential Presidents the equally high distribution of decency, moderation, and dedication to promoting constitutional values." Loss (1976, p. 78) goes on to point out that "President Nixon [in invading Cambodia and covering up Watergate] merely maximized his 'effective influence' as Neustadt had recommended." He acknowledges Neustadt's assertion, in other writings, that the Nixon "regime" was the most corrupt in history, but opines that this is as close as Neustadt

comes to subordinating "effective influence" to political morality, concluding that Neustadt's sole intention is to demonstrate the reasonableness of being favorably disposed toward presidential power (1976, p. 80): "In sum, Neustadt inadequately links the maximization of presidential power to a larger purpose, the benefit of the country, partly because his burrowing into presidential technique as perceived by the White House staff hides the void where a democratic understanding of government should be."

2. The cases of Eisenhower, Coolidge, Taft, and Harding make the point that certain kinds of people (Barber calls them Passive-Positives and Passive-Negatives) respond to frustration by withdrawing from, or avoiding conflict. Other presidents—like Grover Cleveland—behaved with restraint on certain matters as much because of constitutional scruples as because of character-rooted impulse. But, as Barber (1977, p. 145) contends: "The passive Presidents may be a vanishing breed. By my estimation, there has been only one passive president since Calvin Coolidge, [Eisenhower] and his case is a mixed one. Possibly the public senses that rapid change requires an active President." Character can make a difference, then, but it seems that the range of character types have unequal access to the White House. Whatever the reasons, we get more aggressive than nonaggressive presidents.

. . . Perhaps there is some way, without major procedural reform, to help the existing institutions acquire the vision and the will to see to it that we get quality Presidents. I see the most promising development along this line in the steady improvement of data and theory by which present-day decision-makers can predict, if not the "great" Presidents, at least the disastrous ones.

BARBER, *The Presidential Character*

The president is a person. The weight of tradition makes it highly unlikely that the executive agency will ever be directed by any entity other than a single human being. If there is little hope for major change, then we must develop ways of forecasting, with as much accuracy and precision as we can muster, how given individuals will respond to and behave in the presidency. At the very least, we must determine whether we can predict, with better than chance accuracy, how a man or woman will perform as president. And we must consider which of the alternative ways of approaching this problem brings us closer to its solution.

In Search of The Philosopher-King

7

BARBER'S CHARACTEROLOGY

What difference does it make who is president? The clearest and most systematic answer thus far is offered by James David Barber in his widely influential book, *The Presidential Character: Predicting Performance in the White House* (1977).

Barber's basic methodological strategy for developing predictive power can be divided into three stages: (1) Search for and identify the *patterns* in the behavior of past presidents; (2) on the basis of these patterns, classify past presidents into character "types"; (3) predict that a presidential candidate whose known behavior tendencies justify his classification into one or another of the "types" will, in response to similar situations, behave like his characterological predecessors.

There is thus an implicit "stimulus-organism-response" model imbedded in Barber's approach. The stimulus, of course, is the presidency. Barber (1977, p. 5) says that the presidency brings to bear on the president "intense moral, sentimental, and quasi-religious pressures which if he lets them can distort his own thinking and feeling." More specifically, Barber (1977, p. 8) classifies the stimulus field, or the environment, into two categories: (1) the *power situation*—the support the president has from the public and interest groups, the party balance in Congress, the thrust of Supreme Court opinion set the basic power situation he must deal with; and (2) *the climate of expectations*—the predominant needs thrust up to the president by the people, usually embracing one of three recurring themes—needs for reassurance, for a sense of progress and action, and for a sense of legitimacy.

Intervening between these demands and presidential performance is the organism: the character, world view, and style of the president. Each of these influences how a president responds to the demands. *Style*, the most visible part of the pattern, Barber (1977, p. 7) defines as:

> How the President goes about doing what the office requires him to do—to speak, directly or through media, to large audiences; to deal face-to-face with other politicians, individually and in small, rela-

tively private groups; and to read, write, and calculate by himself in order to manage the endless flow of details that stream onto his desk.

A president's *world view* according to Barber (1977, pp. 7–8):

Consists of his primary, politically relevant beliefs, particularly his conceptions of social causality, human nature, and the central moral conflicts of the time. This is how he sees the world and his lasting opinions about what he sees.

World view develops in adolescence, style in early adulthood, and *character*, which for Barber comes in four varieties, has its main development in childhood.

Character is conceived in terms of two intersecting dimensions: active-passive, on the one hand, and positive-negative on the other. The first dimension describes the amount of energy a man invests in the job; the second how he feels about what he does. Barber (1977, p. 12) contends that these two dimensions stand for "two central features of anyone's orientation toward life." The intersecting dimensions yield four character "types": *active-positive*—this is the model American character, the contemporary "Philosopher-King." In Barber's judgment, such a type is temperamentally best suited to the presidency. Characterologically, the active-positive is congruent: he makes intense efforts and he enjoys his work. This type values productiveness and is flexible and growth oriented. His goals are clear. And he has one critical personal resource none of the other types possesses—high self-esteem—which puts him on relatively equal terms with the demands of the presidency. Presidents Barber judges to be active-positive include FDR, Truman, JFK, Ford, and Carter.

The *active-negative* type is, on the other hand, the least desirable and most dangerous character to serve in the presidency. Such people strive mightily for political success, but find the effort punishing and emotionally unsatisfying. Their behavior has a compulsive quality, as if in compensation for feelings of inadequacy. The highest value is to get and keep power, and their stance toward the world is aggressive and hostile. When frustrated, this type digs in and refuses to yield, often bringing disaster on himself and on the political system as a result. To yield to opposition is to acknowledge the truth of their worst fears about themselves—that they're weak and inadequate. The presidents so labeled include Wilson, Hoover, LBJ, and Nixon.

Passive-positives are the "receptive, compliant, other-directed" types, who seek affection as a reward for being agreeable and cooperative rather than personally assertive. This type has low self-esteem but maintains a hopeful, optimistic facade as a way of controlling his doubts and of eliciting affection and encouragement from others. His optimism is a superficial ploy. As presidents, such people pose the danger of drift, because they find it hard to resolve value conflicts decisively. Taft and Harding are the only twentieth century presidents who fit this mold.

Passive-negatives have consistent characters; that is, they do little and enjoy it less. They too are low in self-esteem, but they compensate for this by seeking opportunities to perform useful services. Service in politics helps to quell their feelings of uselessness. Barber argues that these people lack the experience, flexibility, and initiative to perform effectively as political leaders. They are conflict avoiders who cope by withdrawing or by emphasizing vague principles and the importance of rules. As Barber (1977, p. 13) puts it: "They become guardians of the right and proper way, above the sordid politicking of lesser men." Barber supplies case studies of Coolidge and Eisenhower as examples of this type, and notes in passing that George Washington fits here as well.

Table 5 summarizes the chains of influence as represented in Barber's schema. Character, world view, and style interact with the

Table 5   Barber's Approach to Predicting Presidential Behavior

STIMULUS	ORGANISM	RESPONSE
Power situation	Character	Presidential behavior
Climate expectations	World view	
	Style	

power situation and the climate of expectations to produce behavior which, in the case of individual presidents, Barber implies will be consistent with the basic orientations displayed by past presidents.

INTERPRETATION: ACTIVE-POSITIVE OR ACTIVE-NEGATIVE

Barber makes no claim that his scheme is "scientific" in any exact or rigorous sense. It is a conceptual tool which has accumulated some corroborative evidence in support of its utility. Barber conceives its value as being a way to cut through the complexities to perceive the broad outlines of the relation between presidents and the presidency. His scheme leads us to combine a sense of the demands of the presidency with a feel for the general thrust of the president's personality, which can yield something more than chance predictions of presidential behavior, but something less than absolute, "astrological" prediction. Barber has received much criticism on scientific grounds, which he argues is "wide of the mark" given his objectives.[1] His claim to attention rests not with the scientific precision of his scheme, but with his broadly accurate "prediction" that Richard Nixon would be led by his character into destructive and self-defeating behavior as president.

Barber's work is of interest here for two reasons. First, his book is the clearest statement yet rendered of the long-standing American faith in presidential character as the surest solution to the problems of the presidency. He well represents the belief that the problems are best resolved, not by changing the office, but by finding the right person for the job.[2]

Second, Barber does more than anyone else has yet done about the problem of how to identify the most suitable and the least suitable candidates for the presidency. His active-positive and active-negative types identify reasonably clear and straightforward criteria for spotting the best and the worst, respectively. As he puts it (Barber, 1977, p. 445):

[The book's message is] look to character first. At least by the time
the man emerges as an adult, he has displayed a stance toward his
experience, a proto-political orientation. The first clues are simple:
By and large, does he actively make his environment, or is he
passively made by it? And how does he feel about his experience—is
his effort in life a burden to be endured or an opportunity for personal
enjoyment?. . .The lives of Presidents past and of the one(s) still
with us show, I think, how a start from character makes possible a
realistic estimate of what will endure into a man's White House
years.

Of Richard Nixon, the prototypical active-negative president, Barber (p. 459) says:

Nixon demonstrated the vulnerability of the American political system. Throughout his career, his repeated victories after disastrous de-
feats show with dramatic clarity how the process of evaluating potential Presidents failed miserably to predict and guard us from the
machinations of an expert flim-flam man. The American people had
every opportunity to know what they were getting. They elected
Nixon despite the most abundant evidence ever available regarding
the character of any Presidential candidate.

And of Jimmy Carter, the active-positive incumbent, Barber (p.
535) opines:

I believe he will turn out to be a pleasured President, finding, as did
FDR and HST and JFK, that life in the Oval Office can be fun—is on
the average. He has taken the unusual step of writing his own au-
tobiography, a precedent, one hopes, for all future Presidential aspir-
ants. In it he recounts remembered reactions of normal joy,
punctuated to be sure with crises of the spirit. But he dwells on the
pleasures, the positive possibilities, as he did in his boyhood list of
"Healthy Mental Habits." He will be an active-positive President.

Between these bookends fall the passive presidents—the Tafts,
Coolidges, and Eisenhowers. But if, as Barber suspects, the passive
presidents belong to an earlier age,[3] and if, as the literature on polit-

ical recruitment suggests, politics attracts active, ambitious people who are driven by the need to compensate for feelings of inadequacy (the active-negative) or by the pleasure of using their competence to achieve socially valued results (the active-positive), then our future choices appear limited to either power seekers or overachievers, as represented by Nixon and Carter, respectively.

The basic difference between these types seems to rest with how each copes with frustration. Both are aggressive; but the active-positive, says Barber, is less likely to cling stubbornly to a failing course of action, less likely to be goaded by bitterness and power hunger into acts of political suicide, such as those committed by Wilson, Hoover, LBJ, and Nixon. The active-positive is able to put discretion ahead of his urge to prevail, and is capable of backing off to cut his losses. Most important, he knows when to do so.

In a concession that supports one of the major themes of my own argument, Barber (p. 536) acknowledges that active-positives are not totally free of potentially dangerous tendencies:

> Like the other active-positive Presidents, his [Carter's] character-based troubles are going to spring from an excess of an active-positive virtue: the thirst for results. The temptation to go ahead and get some high thing done by some temporary low route may swing him off course, as with Roosevelt and the Court, Kennedy and the Castro problem.

Barber also acknowledges another point that has been stressed repeatedly throughout these pages: that all presidents—all people for that matter, including active-positives—are motivated by the desire to enhance the self. Nowhere does Barber contend that the active-positive has detached himself from the drive toward self-validation. Though his values are more likely to infuse moral and altruistic considerations into his decisions, his hunger for results, and, I would add, the socialization effects of the presidency, are capable of encouraging self-indulgent or self-serving behavior, behavior which can treaten democratic, stability survival, or effectiveness values. Such behavior has occurred before, and it can be expected to occur again.

The basis for Barber's faith in the active-positive character, then, does not rest on any naive claim that the type is immune to, or set apart from, self-serving or self-protective tendencies. Rather, it rests with his belief that the active-positive validates himself by doing things that most of us feel will be good for the country. Though like all the rest of us, his motives must, at bottom, remain essentially selfish, he will solve problems, achieve things, and accomplish popular social and political objectives; and when he encounters the inevitable frustrations, he will be less likely than the active-negative to respond with bitter, malevolent, or vindictively inspired aggression. He is less a prisoner of his impulse, better able to persuade, to compromise, and to display some measure of moral restraint as he seeks to implement his ideal self-concept.

Barber's scheme is insightful and intuitively plausible. His case studies of past presidents make fascinating and instructive reading. Though he chose not to incorporate it in any explicit way, the research evidence available from social psychology does tend to corroborate his central assertion: that the active-positive (high self-esteem) character is, in fact, psychologically best equipped to cope with the demands of the presidency as described in this book.

In the spirit of the present chapter, which aims to assess fairly what can be expected of character, it will be useful to review the evidence pointing to high self-esteem as a coping resource for the president. If we are obliged to retain the presidency in its historic form, then we must, I will argue, understand why high self-esteem is so critically important, learn how to assess the self-esteem of presidential candidates, and devise means of encouraging high self-esteem individuals to seek the presidency. But we must also recognize and accept its limits. As we will see, the evidence points to high self-esteem, but it also corroborates my oft-repeated warning that character is the Achilles heel of the presidency. For all of his virtues, which are considerable, the active-positive president is still a lone ego in a vulnerable position, still preeminently concerned with validating and protecting himself, and thus still susceptible to the sometimes forceful, sometimes invidious influences of the presidency as I have described them. Even the best of us remain, to some extent, the products—if not the victims—of our experience.

THE UTILITY OF SELF-ESTEEM

There are several reasons why the self-esteem concept can be useful in the effort to anticipate how people will respond to the presidency. First, the concept has generated a considerable body of research—more than any other "mentalistic" construct in psychology, except for intelligence (Wells and Marwell, 1976). Second, the self-esteem concept has usually served as the intervening variable in these studies, which experimentally manipulate stimuli that are comparable to the pressures of the presidency—stimuli like stress, frustration, temptation, and status inequality. These studies show that variations in the level of self-esteem are associated with characteristic patterns of adaptation to such pressures, with high self-esteem subjects usually adapting in functional, undistorted ways, analogous to the patterns displayed by active-positive presidents in response to the pressures of the presidency. There is thus, as we shall see, a good bit of evidence to suggest that the high self-esteem character is better able to confront these pressures on equal terms than the low self-esteem character.

Finally, the value of the self-esteem concept is enhanced by its status as an integral part of the explanatory framework found in *self-concept theory*, an increasingly influential body of contemporary personality literature (see Wylie, 1974; Hall and Lindzey, 1970; Gordon and Gergen, 1968). As an explanatory system, self-concept theory may be viewed as an alternative to Barber's characterology, though Barber incorporates many of its assumptions in his case analyses of individual presidents. In my effort to show why high self-esteem is the key coping resource, I will depend more on self-concept theory than on Barber's characterology, for three reasons. First, self-concept theory has been more fully developed, and thus has more systematic explanatory power. Second, because of its relation to the empirical self-esteem literature, self-concept theory has more grounding in research. Third, because self-concept theory evolved in part from research showing how people respond to environmental pressures, it makes for a better "fit" with the psychological environment of the presidency as described in Chapter 2, which, unlike Barber, takes an ahistorical approach to conceptualizing environmental "press." [4]

SELF-CONCEPT THEORY

What is a self-concept? As the term is used here, it can be equated with the conscious sense of identity, with what Tiedeman and O'Hara (1963, p. 17) call "the accumulated meaning one forges about himself as a consequence of his commerce with society." As Eric Erickson (1968) notes, identity is a psycho-social process, "located" in the core of the individual, but also in the core of his environment. That is, the very concept of "self" or "identity" involves the environment as a pervasive actuality. There is no identity—no self—without a sustaining and reinforcing environment. Berger and Luckman (1967) concur in noting that the self is a reflected entity—the individual becomes what he is addressed as by significant others. Identity, they say, is objectively defined as a location in a certain world, and can be subjectively appropriated only along *with* that world.

The importance of the external world to the construction and maintenance of identity, then, helps to explain why people and presidents can be *influenced*—shaped and socialized—by the environment. But people are not, as Greenstein (1975) notes, mere creatures of their environs, passively accepting identities that are thrust upon them. Rather, they are strongly motivated, from the inside, to seek favorable identities.

Self-concept theorists typically posit self-enhancement, or self-validation, as the central, underlying motive of human personality (Wells and Marwell, 1976, p. 54; Hall and Lindzey, 1970, p. 590). A person seeks, in effect, to wrest meaning about himself from the outside world, meaning that he values, and of which he can feel proud. So strong is this need for a positive self-concept that when people are unable to obtain favorable environmental cues (positive feedback), they often invent their own (e.g., self-delusions).

What kind of external evidence, or positive feedback, is capable of validating the self-concept and increasing self-esteem? Evidence which pertains to the satisfaction of two intrinsic human needs, which can be thought of as the major subdivisions of the fundamental need for self-validation: the need for growth (e.g., achievement, efficacy, mastery, self-actualization, competence motivation), and the need for relatedness (e.g., affiliation, love, approval, acceptance). Both the self-concept and self-esteem emerge from a person's lifelong efforts to obtain satisfaction for his growth and relatedness needs. As Freud argued many years ago, the wellsprings of human sustenance and psychological health are work and love (Hall, 1954). A positive self-concept and high self-esteem emerge from and are sustained by the demonstrated ability to satisfy growth and relatedness needs in commerce with the task environment (the world of work) and the interpersonal environment (the world of people). High self-esteem thus implies considerable historical success in getting one's needs met. One has found stable ways of maximizing his well-being—the core routines that sustain his psychological health.

By early adulthood, an individual has crystallized his methods for seeking satisfaction of his growth and relatedness needs. I will call these methods his *behavioral style*—his characteristic ways of relating to the tasks and persons of his chosen (or discovered) environment. Also crystallized by this time are his modes of psychological adjustment—that is, his way of mediating between his internal feeling states and the external realities he confronts (i.e., his psychological style). His behavioral style embodies the skills and techniques he has developed for getting his needs met. His *psychological style* can be viewed as his internal adjustment to the consequences of his behavioral style. That is, if his behavioral style has succeeded (i.e., he is consistently able to satisfy his needs), his psychological style is likely to be nondefensive, reality-based, and relatively objective. If, on the other hand, his behavioral style yields *inadequate* satisfaction (by his own standards) for his growth and relatedness needs, his psychological style is likely to be defensive and/or compensatory—aimed at protecting him from the hostile and unyielding world in which he lives. Psychological style, then, pertains to those crystallized psychological dispositions—beliefs, attitudes, values, aspirations—that serve specific functional purposes for the individual. They help him to adjust to, to comprehend, to defend himself against, or to express himself in relation to his environment (Katz, 1963).

With these distinctions before us, we can see that the self-concept embodies the skills and established competencies of the behavioral style, as well as the most central values and attitudes of the psychological style. We are what we can do, and we strive to become what we value. The more one can do (relative to the performance of significant others), the more respect and affection one can generate; and the closer one's striving behavior approximates his personal ideals, values, and aspirations, the greater will be his self-esteem.

It will be useful to define the terms "value" and "attitude" more explicitly. *Values* are things worth doing and things worth being. The concept corresponds roughly to Barber's "world view" and Alexander George's discussion of "belief system," but is preferred here because it places greater emphasis on the personal utility of judgmental stances. Milton Rokeach's (1973) distinction between *instrumental* and *terminal* values is useful for our purposes. *Instrumental* values are the moral rules of the game. They embody codes of behavior—honesty, integrity, equality—how one should treat others. *Terminal* values, on the other hand, define idealized end-states (e.g., a world of peace, personal salvation) and the more specific and substantive personal aims (such as being president, or other career goals) that can facilitate contribution to ideal end-states. Both kinds of values are judgmental yardsticks applied to others and to the self. Self-esteem is strongly influenced by one's ability to behave consistently with his values and to work toward the goals they embody (Rokeach, 1973). Rokeach argues that violation of instrumental values usually induces anguish or remorse, with direct negative consequences for self-esteem. They are thus particularly important as internalized controls on behavior—a fact of special importance in the context of the presidency.

Attitudes are entrenched functional judgments about specific, cognitive objects (e.g., other people, events, political issues) that enable an individual to explain, adjust, protect, or express himself in relation to such objects. Both attitudes and values protect the self-esteem of all persons. But as noted, they tend to be particularly defensive or compensatory in low self-esteem persons, functioning, for example, as substitutes for adequate need satisfaction (e.g., grandiose aspirations) or protection against one's inability to satisfy his own needs (e.g., displacement of blame onto scapegoats).

These, in brief and simplified form, are the constructs that help to explain how the self-concept emerges, how it functions as an agent for transacting with the outside world, and how it orients itself toward, and protects itself against, the experience presented by that world.

It should now be clearer just why self-esteem is of such critical importance in the presidency—why Barber, implicitly at least, conceives it to be the central coping resource for presidents. Because self-esteem is a consequence of the lifelong process of personality development, it is a relatively stable (i.e., chronic) trait which can serve as a useful summary index of the success of lifelong person-environment interaction. And it can serve as a reasonably good predictor of how an individual might respond to future life experience. In general, *low* self-esteem (e.g., Barber's active-negatives and passive-negatives and positives) implies, according to Wells and Marwell (1976, pp. 70, 72) maladaptation in one form or another:

. . .The person with low self-esteem is more likely to lack self-confidence, be dependent on others, be shy, be nonexplorative and guarded, to use defensive facades. . .be unimaginative, value conformity, avoid self-analysis, and use repressive defenses. . .to be less creative, less flexible. . .*more authoritarian*. . .self-derogating. . .and to be *more disposed toward various forms of deviance*[emphasis mine].

Furthermore:

> Published research indicates fairly decisively that low self-esteem
> persons are more likely to exhibit anxiety and neurotic behaviors
> . . .to *perform less effectively under stress and failure*. . .and to be
> less socially effective overall [emphasis mine].

Conversely, *high* self-esteem (e.g., Barber's active-positive) is associated with "good" or "successful" adjustment, in both the
theoretical and the research literature (Wells and Marwell, 1976, p.
70), suggesting a stable integration of values, attitudes, and needs
around consistently satisfying relationships with the interpersonal
and task environments. According to Sniderman (1975, p. 114):

> . . .Whatever the measure, those judged to be high in self-esteem
> tend to feel confident and sure of themselves; they tend to be more
> optimistic, more likely to believe they can and will succeed; on the
> whole they have confidence in others as well as themselves; they tend
> to feel at ease in the company of others, to have strong supportive
> personal relationships and to be active and self-assertive.

It is the convergently validated existence of such perceptual and behavioral syndromes that argues for the explicit use of the self-esteem
concept in explaining or anticipating responses to self-relevant
stimuli like the pressures of the presidency.

In order to make this point, it will be necessary to reintroduce the
pressures, temporarily abandon my focus on presidents in general,
and review the evidence concerning the response-propensities of
low versus high self-esteem research subjects as they confront such
pressure. I will try to show that presidents lacking in self-esteem
(e.g., Barber's active and passive-negatives and passive-positives)
are more likely to display variants of the "undesirable" behaviors
described in Chapters 3, 4, 5, and 6, and depicted in Tables 1 (p.
42), 2 (61), 3 (85), and 4 (109), than presidents possessed of
high self-esteem (e.g., Barber's active-positives). I also argue, as I
have throughout these pages, that despite his admittedly greater
capacity to stay on equal terms with the pressures, the active-
positive is not immune to their influence.

STRESS AND FRUSTRATION

We can consider stress and frustration simultaneously for two reasons. First they "touch" the president in similar ways. Both confront him with the possibility of failure for which he will be held personally responsible. Both thus pose threats to his professional and public reputations, to his self-concept, and, ultimately, to his self-esteem. Confirmation of the president's identity, and his right to the personal and professional respect of important others, is heavily contingent on his performance in the "tough" problem areas these categories represent.

Second, stress and frustration are often used interchangeably in the research literature (Costello and Zalkind, 1963). Though I have distinguished the two primarily on the basis of the presence or absence of presidential initiative, in both cases the influence-potential of the stimulus hinges upon the fact that the president is responsible for any outcomes. It is the fact of responsibility that engages the self-concept (Bourne, 1971) and the possibility of failure that threatens it (Lewin, 1936).

Available evidence points to a wide variation in research subjects' responses to chronic stress and frustration, but clearly shows that the cumulative impacts are likely to be more severe and *more negative* for those fitting the low self-esteem category. In the context of self-concept theory, chronic stress may be conceived as posing the threat of failure, or negative feedback. Conflict, controversy, uncertainty, forced choices, determined opposition—all of which are inherent in the mediator—as well as crisis management and the advocacy functions of the presidency, carry with them the very real possibility of failure, and thus threaten the security of the president's identity.

Though neither type is immune to the *anxiety* such threats can stimulate, available research shows clearly that the low self-esteem (SE) character is on the average more vulnerable, as self-concept theory would lead us to expect. To begin with, low SE subjects have been shown to be more dependent on environmental support-signals for feelings of personal adequacy (Mabel and Rosenfield, 1966; Witkin et. al., 1962). Because their historically established self-validation routines have not enabled them to satisfy their growth and relatedness needs consistently, they have not accumulated the "reservoir" of self-esteem that would enable them to achieve a measure of psychological detachment from their current trials. Such reasoning would lead us to expect the results reported by Stotland and his colleagues (1957) that low SE subjects were more responsive to criticism, and Cohen's (1959) finding that such persons are more emotionally *vulnerable* to failure experiences. Fitch's (1970) finding that his sample of low SE subjects were significantly more likely to internalize their failure experiences, that is, to look upon situational failure as evidence of their suspected inadequacies, suggests why the low self-esteem president is more likely to interpret conflict, uncertainty, or opposition as a grave threat to his standing. These are the reasons why it is realistic to expect the low SE president to display such adaptive patterns as indiscriminant vigilance (Janis and Leventhal, 1968), excessive energy consumption (Plesur, 1974; Coleman, 1960), physical deterioration, and a long-run decline in performance effectiveness (Child and Waterhouse, 1953) with *greater frequency* than high self-esteem presidents. And indeed, the recent presidents who have responded in these ways have been characterized by psychologically sensitive biographers as possessing low self-esteem: Eisenhower (Barber, 1977); Nixon (Barber, 1977; Mazlish, 1972); Lyndon Johnson (Kearns, 1976); and Wilson (George and George, 1956).

Barber posits three types of low SE presidents, and there is evidence suggesting at least two modal low SE responses to stress and frustration. Their psychological styles appear to distinguish the active-negative, on the one hand, from passive-positives and passive-negatives, on the other. Research suggests that low SE subjects similar to Barber's active-negatives employ expressive ego-defenses, such as projection and regression (Cohen, 1959). In *projection* the ego (self) attributes the threats it feels to external sources rather than in fair measure to their *internal* (e.g., id or superego) sources. Cohen argues that such defensive styles work to sensitize the individual to environmental stimuli and make him more vulnerable to external events. *Regression*, definable as any flight from controlled or realistic thinking in response to an environmental challenge, motivates aggressive or otherwise intemperate responses. The danger is, as Barber argues, that such presidents are especially prone to interpret external frustration as a denial of self and destiny, and are more likely to move to engage and defeat their tormentors. Too, they are generally more likely to view self-vindication as the highest operative value in any given conflict situation.

Passive-positives and negatives, on the other hand, appear from Barber's descriptions to be conflict avoiders who choose avoidance defenses like reaction-formation and repression. *Reaction formation* is defending oneself against anxiety by expressing the opposite of what one really feels, as when excessive altruism masks selfishness, piety conceals sinfulness, or, as with the passive-positive, protestations of love mask fear and bitterness. *Repression* is a conscious denial of an unconsciously desired or feared object, in order to protect the self from facing that object or any situation that is dangerous or would arouse anxiety. Low self-esteem characters who adopt such defenses are as likely as the active-negative to experience the presidency as a threatening milieu, but because they tend to minimize or deny threats, they are less likely to respond with assertiveness or aggression. Thus, Barber warns of the danger of "drift" with passive-positives, and insufficient flexibility and initiative in the case of passive-negatives. Confronted with stress or frustration, these types internalize their pain, and show its effects by developing diseases of adaptation (e.g., heart trouble, ulcers) rather than by behaving aggressively.

It is interesting to note that Cohen's (1959) research suggests that high self-esteem characters employ avoidance defenses like those just described. This may account, in part, for their greater emotional detachment from, and their ability to respond temperately to, their current trials. Although not denying this possibility, self-concept theory would posit that the central reason for the high SE figure's greater capacity to endure stress and cope with frustration and failure stems from his history of need-satisfying self-validation. For high self-esteem implies well-developed task and interpersonal skills. For example, well-established growth-task routines (e.g., consistent satisfaction for achievement of efficacy needs) imply three skills. The first is *flexibility*—the high SE individual is more likely to possess a varied response-repertoire; he is more likely to have adopted an experimental orientation toward the resolution of difficulties than one less self-confident. Because his life experience has taught him that a variety of efforts must be made before success can be expected, he is more of a moving target, and is less likely to settle prematurely on a rigid stance which can increase stress by inviting the forces of opposition to solidify and concentrate on bringing about his defeat. Franklin D. Roosevelt, whose nondoctrinaire approach to the solution of problems has been widely remarked, comes closest to exemplifying this trait. Presidents like Wilson and Lyndon Johnson, on the other hand, markedly increased the stress they had to endure by taking unnecessarily obdurate stands on the central issues of their times. Seeking comfort from a show of inflexible commitment to their policies, both men instead were broken by the critical deluge their commitments stimulated. The second is *resilience*: The high SE individual has a greater tolerance for setbacks because of the accumulated reservoir of success he has internalized. His successful history gives him a greater store of emotional capital upon which to draw in order to weather difficult periods. His more firmly established sense of efficacy requires less reinforcement to be sustained because it is less contingent on his current performance than is the case with low self-esteem people. Hence, the success rate needed to maintain self-esteem is lower, and resilience in the face of stress, frustration, or failure is correspondingly greater. The third is *detachment*. Because feelings of potency are less dependent on environmental signals (Mabel and Rosenfeld, 1966; Witkin et. al., 1962), and partially because the high SE individual employs avoidance defenses which help him to minimize external threats and to maintain his self-picture at a high level (Cohen, 1959), such a person is able to maintain a certain emotional distance and independence from his current trials. And he is less likely to experience debilitating anxiety or emotional pain under conditions of failure or prolonged stress (Schalon, 1968; Shrauger and Rosenberg, 1970).

Flexibility, resiliance, and detachment can be thought of as *growth skills*—abilities developed in the process of expressing the competence or achievement motive. Additional fortification against stress and frustration is implied by the *interpersonal skills* of the high SE person as well. Sniderman (1975) found that his sample of high self-esteem people was more at ease in the company of others, more likely to have strong, supportive relationships, and generally better equipped to win and maintain the respect and affection of others. The interpersonal skills that can be inferred from self-concept theory, and which are implied by Sniderman's findings, include the ability to establish genuine rapport with others, and a capacity for achieving mutuality, defined as that degree of trust sufficient to ensure that all of the relevant information is exchanged between interacting parties, without recourse to exploitative or self-protective duplicity (Alderfer and Brown, 1975).

The point is that relatedness needs, whose satisfaction is one major precondition for high self-esteem, cannot be satisfied without these abilities. If one is consistently unable to establish rapport and mutuality, he will find it impossible to meet his relatedness needs. Presumably, high self-esteem presidents are better able than their low SE counterparts to be "open" when they need or choose to do so. At least two low SE presidents—Wilson and Nixon—are said to have been unable to establish close relationships without attaching such self-protective conditions as uncritical admiration or unquestioning loyalty (George and George, 1956; Safire, 1975).

The role of interpersonal skills in stress endurance has been suggested by Torrance, a leading figure in stress research (1963). Torrance concludes that a major factor contributing to the endurance of prolonged stress is successful interpersonal relationships. The supportive, comforting, and tension reducing aspects of human interaction serve as antidotes for such effects as anxiety, inconsistent behavior, and breakdown, all of which among the consequences of stress identified by Torrance.

Rapport and mutuality skills enable presidents to draw upon others for emotional support in trying circumstances without fear of revealing inadequacies or weaknesses. Woodward and Bernstein

(1976) report that in the final throes of his Watergate ordeal, Richard Nixon was not candid with his legal counsel, his friends, or even with his family. This is strong evidence of an inability to achieve mutuality, given the enormous stress Nixon was under and his obvious need for emotional support.

Thus, we see that, on balance, the high SE individual enjoys greater psychological protection from stress and frustration than does his low SE counterpart. The ego-defensive aspects of his psychological style lead him to minimize the negativity of his experience, thus detaching himself from some of its pain. In contrast, the low SE individual is much more likely to perceive and internalize such threats. The high SE person has a reservoir of emotional capital, which affords him the psychological comfort and freedom to respond flexibly and resiliently to threats, whereas his low SE counterpart is more likely to rigidify defiantly (active-negative) or withdraw altogether (passive-negative; passive-positive) because he tends to see his own worth as directly and seriously threatened by almost any challenge he confronts. And the high SE figure is more interpersonally competent, which gives him access to the kind of emotional support that can lighten his burden. The low SE character, conversely, finds relationships more difficult, and thus must weather his trials with less support.

With available theory and evidence pointing as clearly and unequivocally as it does to the superior mettle of the high self-esteem figure under fire, the reader is entitled to wonder why I feel compelled to register any doubts about his capacity to avoid the negative influences of stress and frustration. Surely a president as well-adjusted and as psychologically fortified as this can be expected to stay on equal terms with anything the presidency can throw at him?

My answer is—not necessarily. It is hard to dispute the greater capacity of the high self-esteem president to weather chronic stress, but its unrelieved nature—particularly in turbulent times—can strain and drain the hardiest of souls, a point I tried to establish in Chapter 3. I would contend that the main advantage of the active-positive rests with his greater capacity to *endure*—to bear up somewhat longer—before succumbing to withdrawal, self-protective distortions, or diseases of adaptation. But a greater capacity for endurance is by no means equivalent to immunity from stress and its consequences. Recall, for example, the exclamations of active-positive presidents under stress—Harry Truman, John Kennedy, Franklin Roosevelt, and Thomas Jefferson—reprinted in Chapter 3. These presidential expressions of anxious wariness (Truman, p. 35), vindictive anger (Kennedy, p. 38), irritation and exasperation (FDR, p. 38), and exquisite pain (Jefferson, p. 39), make it plain that stress touches and affects such presidents.

My reservations about the frustrated active-positive are even more pronounced. Granted, the high SE president is much less likely to interpret any and all obstacles as denials of his self and his destiny. But recall that the major emphasis of the active-positive— the value in whose service this type validates his worth—is achievement. He is hell-bent on getting things done. We have seen that his sense of worth is, on the whole, less contingent upon successful attainment of his immediate ends. But in the context of the presidency, the number of contested issues a president can safely let slide is sharply restricted.

We must bear in mind that the presidency is *not* an ordinary arena. It is the pinnacle—a setting which, from *any* president's point of view, magnifies the significance of anything that happens to him all out of normal proportion. Unyielding visibility and inescapable responsibility tend—on the average—to invest much more of a president's life space and work experience with identity-relevant meaning—in a sheer *quantitative* sense—than would be the case in any "normal" work environment. Self-concept theory advises us that there is no identity without an environment. But this particular environment has far fewer "safe" spaces, fewer chances to detach and "coast"—to breathe easy—than would be afforded in almost any other demanding job. The margin for error is much smaller, the chances for important failure much greater. To some extent, these factors mitigate against the tendency of high SE figures to limit their intense ego-involvements to a smaller range of truly important issues. Of course, one way of coping with such a milieu is to deliberately restrict the number of issues on which the president publicly stakes his prestige. Presidents routinely seek to do this. And here the active-positive, by dint of his innate proclivities, enjoys an advantage. He may find such a strategy consistent with his impulse. But the presidency remains the supreme vehicle for individual achievement. And active-positives, the prototypical overachievers, will seek to use it this way. And on those matters involving their most cherished aspirations, their fondest hopes for creation, they will not be serenely detached. They will not calmly accept whatever successes the political milieu reluctantly yields.

I think the case of Roosevelt and the Supreme Court, discussed in Chapter 6, makes a telling point in this regard. On matters of profound personal importance to them, matters which engage and channel their achievement energies, and which involve the attainments for which they wish to be remembered, active-positives tend to behave like active-negatives. They may be less likely to interpret every challenge as an intolerable affront. They may be less likely, as Barber argues, to cling stubbornly to an obviously lost cause. But they will respond just as aggressively in areas of great personal importance to them. When caught up in a massive struggle involving conflicts among major values, they, like Franklin D. Roosevelt, can be expected to place a higher value on personal vindication than upon larger, longer-run stability or democratic values. A human being, challenged where he lives, and who feels righteous about his aims, is simply not in a position to measure the values his plans may threaten. He is too entangled in the situation, and has too much at stake, for us to expect this of him. This is neither weakness or malevolence. Rather, it is a normal expression of the bedrock nature of human beings. The mind-set of such a person thus engaged is best captured, I think, in Edmund Burke's empathetic warning that opened Chapter 6 (p. 101).

The political rationale for such behavior, as Barber (1977, p. 536) indicates in his acknowledgment of its possibility, is worthy ends: "the temptation to go ahead and get some high thing done by some temporary low route." Apparently, the tendency of active-positives to invest themselves in aims for which there is broad popular support puts Barber's mind somewhat to rest on this question.

And Barber is not alone. The historical judgments of presidents past—men like Jefferson, Jackson, Polk, and Theodore Roosevelt—reflect the triumph of popular ends over questionable means. Historically, the thirst for results has been countenanced when the ends sought enjoyed sufficient popular support.[5]

My problem with this state of affairs is that even popular presidential initiatives, when not tempered with enforceable scruples about means, can redound in unanticipated and undesirable ways. Returning for a moment to the case of FDR and the Supreme Court, we can note that many liberals who shared Roosevelt's vision for America felt that his righteous determination to prevail was amply justified. Yet had he used his political skill to full effect, he might well have succeeded in altering the Court's composition and changing its historical function. To my mind, his initiative seemed an unnecessary and avoidable threat to the stability and identity of the Court, an institution whose long-term value is at least comparable and perhaps superior to the short-run values its intransigence threatened.

A core assumption of Richard Neustadt's argument in *Presidential Power* (1976) is that a president's pursuit of self-validation (i.e., protecting and promoting his personal power as the highest operative value) "contributes to the energy of government and the viability of public policy." I would respond that while a president's service of his own achievement and power needs can, and often does, coincide with effective service to the larger requirements of the republic, there is no necessary correlation. Neustadt is, I think, correct in his implicit assumption that most presidents will be motivated to protect and enhance their power stakes. But to further assume that such behavior will somehow automatically serve and promote stability, effectiveness, and democratic values is unwarranted, and, I think, dangerous.

DEFERENCE AND DISSONANCE

Returning now to the task of comparing the response propensities of low versus high self-esteem research subjects, our next concern is with variations in response to deference and dissonance. Again, the available evidence points to the superiority of the high self-esteem character in the face of such pressures.

The likelihood that low SE presidents will be particularly susceptible to deference is suggested by the self-esteem literature, which highlights the greater persuasibility (Cohen, 1959); a greater dependence on external support in maintaining feelings of personal adequacy (Mabel and Rosenfeld, 1966); the tendency toward estrangement from all but a small number of trusted and supportive intimates (Sniderman, 1975, p. 97–98); and a greater tendency toward anxiety (Rosenberg, 1965), which impels a greater tendency to seek unquestioning affiliative support (Schacter, 1959) among low SE subjects.

And there is corroborative evidence from the presidency itself. Certain low SE presidents who "fit" Lasswell's compensation hypothesis—active-negatives who display compulsive-aggressive expressions of their low self-esteem, rather than the avoidance expressions characteristic of passive-negatives or passive-positives (see Sniderman, 1975, p. 241)—seem to have been prone to compensatory delusions of grandeur, and thus particularly susceptible to the influence of the kind of overdrawn assessments of their stature encouraged by status inequality. For an illustration of this phenomenon, the reader is referred to the selection from the Georges' study of Woodrow Wilson, reprinted above in Chapter 4 (pp. 59–60). Additional examples are supplied by the behavior of Richard Nixon and Lyndon Johnson described in Chapter 4 (p. 61) and Chapter 5 (p. 86) respectively. Further, both of these men were unusually preoccupied with the symbolic trappings of office—the kind of overidentification with the presidency likely to be associated with both compensatory self-estimates and susceptibility to deference.

As regards dissonance—the lure of expediency—available research evidence is sparse, but it is consistent with the expectation that low self-esteem subjects are more susceptible to situational temptations to misrepresent themselves. The results of one study led its authors to conclude that persons high in self-esteem are less prone than low SE subjects to perform any activities generally dis sonant with their private opinions (Aronson and Mettee, 1968). Employing measures of both chronic and experimentally induced self-esteem, the same study found that significantly more people cheated in the low SE than the high SE condition. Graf (1971) found a similar negative relationship between self-esteem and cheating. And Wright (1971) reviews a variety of studies involving the personal correlates of resistance to temptation which are broadly consistent with these findings.

At least two recent presidents to whom Lasswell's compensation hypothesis has been applied, Johnson and Nixon, displayed a willingness to employ large-scale deception in the service of their aims (Kearns, 1976; White, 1975). Presumably, the association of low self-esteem and persuasibility accounts in part for the greater susceptibility of such presidents to the "right to lie" norms discussed in Chapter 5 (Cohen, 1959; Wise, 1973).

Taken together, the self-esteem studies, plus the consistent behavior of low SE presidents, do suggest that the low SE president is more likely to have his head turned by deference and more likely to fall prey to situational temptations to deceive than his high SE counterpart. How does self-concept theory explain these findings? More specifically, what is the source of the high self-esteem figure's greater resistance to flattery and to situational temptation?

Again, the answer derives from the assumed presence of personal attributes that are taken to be implied by the fact of high self-esteem. Just as high self-esteem implies superior task and interpersonal skills, so too does it imply certain characteristic psychological styles, which, like task and people skills, can be viewed as long-run consequences of historically successful personal development. Most important among these for present purposes are egalitarian and truth values.

Closely associated with the mutuality and rapport skills discussed above are underlying instrumental values which predispose an individual to relate to others in reciprocal ways. High self-esteem implies egalitarian and truth values because need-satisfying relationships cannot be established in the absence of values which place human interaction on a firmly reciprocal, as opposed to an exploitative, dominant, or dependent basis. We would thus expect high SE persons—people who have demonstrated their ability to establish genuine relationships—to have internalized such values as egalitarianism and veracity. As a purely practical matter, reciprocity is best served by values which lead one to respect the views of others and to deal with them openly.

The relevance of such values to coping with deference and dissonance has to do with their status as influencers of perception and internalized controls on behavior. For example, egalitarianism—belief in the fundamental equality of human beings—can mitigate against the distortions of deference by increasing the likelihood that a president's men will deal with him candidly. Any president who truly shares the belief—attributed to Eisenhower (Hargrove, 1974, p. 59)—that "each individual must make up his own mind about right and wrong, and that one must take that right as a given in dealing with people," is more likely to stimulate both candor and realistic give-and-take than one who consciously or unconsciously treats other men as lesser beings, or as objects of suspicion. The climate encouraged by such interaction norms can increase the authenticity of social comparison processes. And because his values make him more approachable, such a president is in a better position to attract counsel from beyond his immediate circle.

Similarly, genuine truth values constitute internal checks against the lure of expedient misrepresentation. Indeed, in the context of the presidency, they are often the only significant checks. If they are central to self-definition, failure to heed them threatens self-respect, something we all fight to protect (Rokeach, 1973).

A president who seemed to embody both egalitarian and truth values was active-positive Harry Truman. Determined, as he put it, to do "what is right," Truman was committed to living his values, and he consistently applied an inner moral yardstick to his actions. This was apparent in his treatment of subordinates and his fondness for outspoken candor, neither of which was an unbridled advantage for him politically. He was often overdeferential toward those he respected, like Secretary of State Byrnes, and General MacArthur, with undesirable consequences both for policy consistency and for his presidential power-stakes. And his arresting candor at press conferences, the delight of reporters, often led him to make policy "on his feet," without adequate reflection (Phillips, 1966). But his record does show a near-total invulnerability to deference and dissonance pressures, best explained, I think, in terms of instrumental moral values.

Once again, then, the available evidence suggests that high self-esteem individuals are better equipped to withstand the pressures. Once again, self-concept theory supplies a plausible explanation. And once again, I feel the need to register important doubts.

Granted, the evidence suggests that high self-esteem presidents will, on the average, resist the influences of deference and dissonance significantly more often than low self-esteem presidents. Granted, psychologically secure and well-nourished people have less need for the obeisance of political "groupies." Granted, such people may feel less frequent need for the cloak of secrecy. They are accustomed to working in the open and might thus be less prone to use the presidency as camouflage.

Once more, however, we come up against the absolutely unique milieu of the presidency. The presidential experience, abetted by the influences of the political culture through which virtually all successful presidential candidates must pass en route to the White House, further reinforced by the norms and mores of the highest policy councils, and cemented, as it were, by the expectations imbedded in the traditions of the dominant presidency, are collectively able to override character and to overpower it. The reinforcement patterns to which presidents are subjected—what gets rewarded and what gets punished—are quite capable, as we have seen, of inducing active-positives to depart from their natural tendencies. Such recent evidence as is available—the Alker study (1976) of presidential deception, FDR's behavior in the Supreme Court incident, and JFK's secret war on Castro—establishes the point that active-positives do sometimes employ guile, duplicity, and secrecy. This is not moral condemnation on my part. Rather, it is my effort to show that the environment of the presidency selects this kind of behavior, and operates to extinguish the kind of straightforward, square-shooting displayed by Harry Truman. Yes, presidents do come along who absolutely refuse to succumb to these aspects of the presidential experience. But they are rare as hen's teeth, near-impossible to spot in advance, and, frankly, unlikely to climb far enough up the political career-ladder to be taken seriously as presidential prospects.

The impact of status inequality upon active-positives will be similarly discernible, though predictably less telling in its consequences than for the various low SE characters. Recall that in Chapter 4 the point was made that no one can achieve total independence from social comparison processes, which are the major means for testing reality and maintaining an objective view of self and externalities. When any person's social comparison processes are consistently and systematically slanted in a supportive direction for a period of four and quite possibly eight years, it seems an inevitable and inescapable fact that he who is so treated will eventually suffer some damage to the objectivity of his interpretations.

True, the high SE figure is more likely to be open, more likely to encourage the unvarnished truth, and consequently more likely to sustain his access to the information and opinion he needs. But let him once lose his temper in the company of those who provide him information (he will). Let him once express his displeasure with the source of an unpleasant truth (he will). Let him show even a fleeting pique with the messenger, and he will have triggered a cue—sent his own message—that will set in motion those editorial forces in the minds of his people that, with the best of intentions, will gradually detach him from what he needs to know. Those around him will do this unthinkingly, automatically, in their eagerness to serve him. The process will be too gradual and too subtle for the president to perceive and take steps to arrest. His status opens up too great a chasm between his people and himself to expect anything else. We can concede that an active-positive's problems in this area will be predictably less severe. But his human dependence on the interpretations of others, plus the subtlety of the workings of status inequality, effectively rule out any possibility that he can be impervious to this kind of influence.

CONCLUSION: NO SECURE SOLUTION

Where does this leave us? In hearty agreement with Barber. Given the status quo, we are well advised to recruit and select only high self-esteem presidents. The coping patterns of such persons are demonstrably superior, across a variety of experimental and social situations, to those of low SE persons. If the presidency must remain as it is—as most readers are likely to feel—then the agenda is clear. Despite the qualifications I have offered, there is no serious question about the greater suitability of the active-positive. The problem then becomes, as the self-esteem literature makes abundantly clear, one of measurement. No widely accepted index of self-esteem has established itself, and there is great disagreement among measurement specialists concerning how to assess this attribute. [6] Such disagreement does not justify abandoning the concept, however, because regardless of how it is measured, self-esteem routinely correlates with adaptive patterns in ways that point to the superior capacities of high self-esteem subjects. [7] But developing valid and reliable assessment techniques—techniques which can be understood and applied by the great majority of citizens—is an essential next step. Barber's dimensions of activity and affect are an important, if incomplete, step in this direction. And, as Barber argues in the quotation that began the present chapter, this is compelling work.

But I hope it is also clear that this course of action involves significant problems—problems it is incumbent upon those who would retain the historical presidency in its traditional form to recognize, and, where feasible, to solve.

There is first a series of problems associated with ensuring a regular supply of active-positive presidential candidates. The barriers are significant. One is the fact that high self-esteem is a scarce commodity. High self-esteem personalities are almost as rare as Plato's elusive Philosopher-Kings—a fact that Plato recognized by conceiving lifelong development programs for producing them. By the estimates of psychologists, as little as one-fourth of the population has developed this personal resource (Branden, 1971). Another barrier has to do with the traditional presidential selection process. As matters stand, no part of that process concerns itself with character in any systematic way, save perhaps for citizens on election day. And so far as we can tell, active-positives may be underrepresented in the "applicant pool" taken most seriously by political professionals and the public. Though research has generated no clearcut agreement as to the "types" of personalities attracted to political careers (Di Renzo, 1974), the political recruitment literature does converge upon the identification of various "pathological" characteristics, like compensatory power-striving (George, 1972; Browning and Jacob, 1964) and authoritarianism (Di Renzo, 1974), as being overrepresented in political life.

Recent national experience—and common sense—tell us that those who make the final presidential sweepstakes are men of near-fanatical personal ambition who show themselves willing to sacrifice health, family, peace of mind, and principle, in order to win the prize. To the question, "What price, success?" presidential candidates are near-unanimous in responding: "Any price." This kind of preoccupation with personal success—absolutely necessary for attaining the presidency in the present era—is neither characteristic of, nor does it favor the prospects of, moderate or temperate people. Rather it suggests that aggressive types—some positive, some negative—will prevail. The selection process works to anoint the most vigorous, the most resilient, and the most aggressive.[8] Barber argues plausibly that in combination with moral restraint, such qualities are to be desired. But this returns us to the problem of assessment. How are we to know for sure who's positive and who's negative? Jimmy Carter, whom Barber calls positive, has displayed some naggingly negative traits all along his path to political success.[9] At the very least, the Carter case illustrates the fine powers of discrimination needed to spot the "quality" candidates.

Last is the fact that those who would leave things just as they are must recognize and accept the inevitability of recurring trouble. Whether active-positive or active-negative, the safest prediction I can make is that the centrality of the lone ego in our most critical political institution will in the future result in threats or damage to democracy, to effectiveness, or to stability values. We have been lucky—luckier than the probabilities suggest we can expect to be in the future.

To some, reliance on presidential character may seem a calculated risk which, on balance, is worth the candle, particularly in light of the considerable uncertainties and risks associated with any major structural or procedural reform. To me, the near-inevitability of future trouble, brought on by the responses of solitary human beings to the presidential experience, constitutes sufficient grounds for looking closely at what might be done to reduce the impact of the presidential experience. As we shall see, there are no panaceas at hand. Rather, there might be some workable and politically feasible changes, capable of improving the probabilities. Given the fact that character can offer no secure solution, it is only prudent that we look for ways to supplement it.

NOTES

1. Among Barber's most thoroughgoing critics are Alexander George (1974) and James H. Qualls (1977). Among other things, George finds fault with Barber's failure to establish the comparability of situations. That is, before Barber can claim that similar presidential behavior implies similar character, he must establish that the situational stimulation faced by each compared president was similar enough to be taken as controlled. In other words, one must control for the situation before he can attribute behavior to character. Otherwise, similar behavior might be induced by the situation rather than by character. Qualls, on the other hand, faults Barber for his overemphasis on character, relative to world view and style, as explanatory constructs (a point George makes as well). Qualls also provides an elaborate methodological critique of the assessment techniques employed by Barber in his book, *The Lawmakers* (1965), on the supposition that the coding scheme used in the earlier study informed the typology of presidential character employed in the 1972 study. Qualls concludes that the reliability and validity of Barber's classification decisions are severely flawed. For his own part, Barber (1977b, p. 225) dismisses both sets of criticisms as "creating nothing but a false sense of the possibilities of per-

fection.'' In a stinging retort to his critics, Barber (1977b, pp. 213, 223, 225) notes that neither of his books "is offered as some mathematical, mechanical, or definitive treatment of the subject," deplores those who are given to requiring "abstract criteria neither [they] or any other researcher into these matters has ever met," and laments the "grim trivialization of political science by naive technicians."

2. An earlier statement of this faith is supplied by William Penn (quoted in Corwin, 1957, p. 31):

   When all is said, there is hardly any frame of government so ill-designed by its founders that in good hands would not do well enough; and story tells us the best in ill ones, can do nothing that is great or good. . . .Governments, like clocks, go from the motion men give them; and as governments are made and moved by men, so by them they are ruined too. Therefore governments rather depend upon men than men upon governments.

3. See Chapter 6, footnote 2.

4. See Chapter 1, footnote 10.

5. As Rexford Tugwell (1960, p. 93) observes in his discussion of the Jackson presidency: "The politician has a kind of rationalizing mechanism others find it difficult to understand. It has no necessary relation to reason; it need not be consistent with any pattern; it need only be approved by a majority of the voters—this is regarded as complete vindication."

6. For a compendium of measures of self-esteem and the self-concept, plus critical comparative reviews of the measures, see Ruth C. Wylie, *The Self Concept*, revised edition, Volume One, University of Nebraska Press, 1974.

7. See Sniderman quote, this chapter, p. 138.

8. And, it might be added, to one who has successfully endured this most rigorous of exercises in self-promotion, the presidential experience can hardly be expected to allay his so recently elicited and reinforced self-protective and self-promoting tendencies.

9. Carter's critics point to his preference for the company of a small band of like-minded intimates, his reluctance to compromise, his extreme competitiveness and occasional vindictiveness, as signs of the kind of negativity that Barber attributes to the active-negative character. Reg Murphy, former editor of the *Atlanta Constitution*, opines: "If politics is the art of the possible, Jimmy Carter won't get along with anybody in Washington, because he is a mean, hardeyed sort of fellow who tol-

erates nobody who opposes him. The Governor just absolutely does not take challenges from anybody" ("Carter Up Close," *Newsweek*, July 19, 1976, p. 23). And in explaining why he abandoned a sure victory in the race for a Congressional seat in order to run against Bo Callaway for the Governorship of Georgia, Carter (1975, p. 110) himself acknowledges: "In retrospect, it is difficult to assess all my reasons. Although it is not especially admirable, one of the major reasons was a natural competitiveness with Bo Callaway."

Given the history of failure of past efforts, both from within Congress and from outside it, to effect fundamental changes. . .the prospects appear to be practically nil. Change in a fundamental sense is likely to occur only if some great catastrophe in the nation's life—such as, God forbid! an all-out nuclear war, or an internal upheaval. . .should befall us.

KALLENBACH, "The Presidency and the Constitution: A Look Ahead"

Proposals for reforming the presidency have surfaced and been debated since 1789. Ours is a society that likes to tinker with and improve its machinery—political machinery included. Americans, perhaps more than most other peoples, thrive on change, talk about it constantly, and create it almost as often. But despite a bewildering variety of specific proposals for change, backed by an equally impressive array of rationales, reasons, and justifications, they have never shown themselves willing to change the presidency. Even after Vietnam and Watergate—presidential setbacks without peer in American history—the reform impulse quickly abated. The presidential institution remains an impregnable fortress, an enduring

THE PRESIDENTIAL EXPERIENCE: Antidotes

8

158

monolith, a cornerstone of our national identity, an immutable "sacred cow."

There are good reasons for this—reasons we should have in mind before looking at the proposals for change that are suggested by my analysis of the presidential experience. First and most important among the barriers to change is the fact that the presidency works. Despite inglorious moments, intermittent failures and setbacks, the presidency has performed tolerably well for two centuries. In the hands both of great and less than great presidents, it has embodied our values, reconciled our domestic conflicts, posed workable solutions to our national problems, and coped with sudden emergencies. From its inception, the presidency has been beset with troubles. Hostile and aggressive neighbors early on. The constant threat and the occasional fact of invasion by more powerful European states. Unrelenting and sometimes disastrous internal squabbling, first over economic advantage, next the taming of the continent, then slavery, culminating in one of the most futile and self-destructive civil wars ever fought. Periodic economic ruin, two World Wars of terrifying proportions, the emergence of the United States as a major world power, the creation of electronic and nuclear technology, an ominous cold war, and a host of other crises and milestones—any one of which might have disrupted less hardy or less effective political institutions. Somehow we are alive, well, and in more or less recognizable form. Credit for this belongs in no small measure to the historical presidency.[1]

The next barrier to change is the fact of a truly special psychological relationship between the presidency and the American people. The traditional presidency has burrowed deeply into the American psyche, and sparked there a visceral and abiding trust in the institution—a trust that apparently cannot be destroyed by an occasional miscreant president. Indeed, the hold of the historical presidency on the minds of the people may well be the single most important reason for the political stability that distinguishes this government from most others. The power of the president and the presidency to mobilize and galvanize the people into facing and coping with emergent problems derives importantly from this visceral trust. It is thus a resource of inestimable value. As the experience of other governments attests, such a bond is not easily created. And it is not lightly to be bartered away. Any major change in the historical presidency could threaten this relationship, and leave a massive and complex society without compass or rudder.

To these barriers must be added the costs and uncertainties associated with major change. Any reform significant enough to alter the traditional functioning of the presidency is also significant enough to provoke anxiety and unrest in the minds of citizens. The fluid, unpredictable situation that would obtain while new arrangements were being implemented and tested might trigger fear or panic. Even minor mistakes could produce an abrupt loss of faith in the shaky new arrangements.

Then there is the added uncertainty of whether or not the adopted changes—seemingly prudent and workable on paper—would in fact perform as expected. The framers of the Constitution would be amazed and perhaps dismayed at how their plans turned out in practice. So, too, might the long-term consequences of reform prove to be substantially different from expectations—and perhaps substantially worse. Responsible minds, comparing a flawed but workable status quo with an unknown ideal, cannot be faulted for their reluctance to jeopardize the familiar in order to test rosy sounding but unpredictable reforms.

This litany of obstacles helps to make the point that any major change in the presidency will be resisted and would be fraught with significant peril. Most people feel that it is too risky to tamper with the presidency or with any of our other institutions. Winning political support for major change borders on the impossible, and any discussion of reform must come squarely to grips with this fact. As Kallenbach observes in the opening quote, only a catastrophe of some sort is likely to pave the way for change. Why, then, close this book with a chapter on reform?

Because of the presidential experience. The central purpose of this book has been to show that the presidency has an impact on presidents. And that, on balance, this impact is more than acceptably dangerous to any president's ability to perform effectively, to his respect for democratic values, and ultimately to the stability of our political arrangements. Presidents are conditioned—by the repetition and force of the four exposures described in this book—in ways that (1) deplete their physical and emotional energy; (2) nurture systematic distortions in the accuracy with which they perceive themselves and external events; (3) encourage the use of duplicity as an expedient political resource; and (4) erode any values or scruples that interfere with the preservation of presidential power. These exposures encourage behavior like indiscriminate vigilance, isolation, irrational decision-making, outright lying, arrogations of power, and provocations of conflict with the other branches of government. Behaviors like these have undermined presidential effectiveness, done violence to constitutional processes and democratic values, and threatened to disrupt political stability in the past. Since the dynamics of influence that encourage such behavior remain intact, the probabilities point to future threats to effectiveness, democracy, and stability values. The presidential institution thus carries within it self-destructive tendencies—tendencies we would do well to dilute, alter, or remove.

A skeptical reader might ask, how urgent is this problem? With Watergate and Vietnam safely behind us, no disaster appears to lurk on the horizon. We have a new man in office, and some presidents seem to have successfully resisted the ravages of stress, deference, dissonance, and frustration altogether. Why get excited when, in theory at least, it is possible to spot people able to tolerate, endure, or even enjoy the job without falling prey to the distortions. By now we should know enough to spot and avoid the disasters, while electing suitable characters much more often than we have in the past. In any case, it is perhaps better to risk an occasional misfit than to redesign an historically successful office.

Furthermore, the presidential experience works in gradual and subtle ways, analogous, for the most part, to water dripping on a stone. When presidential troubles and crises do occur, they do not seem to be clearly or unarguably linked to anything so distant as the long-term influences of office. And much of the time—during politically quiet times or uneventful presidencies—the presidential experience recedes into the background. It poses no apparent problem and produces no dramatic or otherwise compellingly obvious impact. There is no sense of urgency. In short, the presidential experience will not be perceived as the kind of catastrophic problem capable of stimulating a public demand for change.

I recognize these things as the barriers to change they are. But I must retort that the apparent subtlety and unobtrusiveness of the presidential experience can be quite deceptive. Let me reiterate a point made in the Preface. Granted, the presidential experience works its influence gradually, over the long haul, while political disaster is usually galvanized by some specific and immediate crisis or event. Granted, there is no simple cause and effect relationship between the pressures and political disaster. But by influencing presidents in the ways described, the pressures increase the likelihood of dangerous responses to specific events. By encouraging certain kinds of behavior, the exposures conduce toward outcomes that threaten our important values. What this means is that things can flash suddenly and unpredictably out of control at any time. For example, the distortions of deference, accumulating without fanfare over time, may contribute to a decision that proves to have sudden, disastrous consequences, like Nixon's decision to fire Archibald Cox. Or a president may succumb to the temptation to hide a key mistake, forget about it, be asked an embarrassing question at a press conference, and find himself forced into a cycle of increasingly risky deceptions. Frustration may cumulate quietly and privately inside a president's skull, unnoticed by the public, and then suddenly erupt in a pitched battle or a secret move to destroy the opposition. Physiological adjustments to stress—unnoticed by outsiders or the president himself—might unexpectedly provoke a presidential heart attack or a stroke. Each of these things has happened before, and each will happen again. Given the potential for damage to our values, it behooves us at least to consider what might be done about the presidential experience.

THE "WHY" OF REFORM

It is worth noting that the perspective on reform taken here is quite different from that usually taken by those who write about changing the presidency. Most would-be change agents have been concerned—in the words of a popular recent text (Cronin, 1975)—either with "making the presidency safe for democracy," or with "making the president an effective executive." My own perspective on reform is that of a systems analyst faced with the problem of maximizing system survival prospects. In systems theory terms, the highest value is long-term survival in recognizable form (von Bertalanffy, 1956). The "system" is the United States, and the threat to its stability and survival is a latent one, posed by the socialization experiences routinely visited upon the person of the central executive.

My central question is: "How can the presidential experience be altered so as to reduce the threat it poses to the long-term stability of the United States government and American society?" We know, of course, that the presidential experience also threatens the president's ability to perform his functions effectively, and tends to undermine his respect for constitutional processes and democratic values. But these are subordinate to stability; they are among the antecedent conditions that must be met if stability and survival are to be ensured. The latter is a more inclusive perspective that helps to clarify in basic and fundamental ways just what it is we seek to preserve and protect—and what might be the best way to go about it. [2] Yes, the president must be an effective executive and he must respect democracy if the system is to endure in perpetuity. But he must also be encouraged or led to avoid sudden, dangerous actions, impetuous decisions, and explosive, no-win situations capable of flashing out of control and reducing us all to rubble. These things are possible and all the more probable because the president is nothing more than a human being. Approaching reform with the idea of increasing democracy or improving effectiveness is not enough. Such perspectives tend to divert attention away from fundamentals and toward such questions as whether or not it is appropriate to look upon the president as a "manager," [3] or to rankings of those groups whose welfare has best been served and protected by the presidency. [4] The question with both ethical and temporal priority is: How does the presidency threaten our survival and what can be done about it?

When presidents mislead the people and get caught at it, when they base major decisions on faulty, distorted information or wishful thinking, when they indulge themselves in breast-thumping battle with other legitimate power centers, and when they risk war to save face, they are posing unacceptable threats to our prospects for long-term stability and survival.[5] These very behaviors are among the expectable consequences of the presidential experience. What might be done about it is the next subject of concern.

ORGANIZING THE OPTIONS

I have acknowledged that political reality places severe limits on the prospects for fundamental change. Table 6 reflects sensitivity to this reality by arranging the reform options noted briefly at the close of earlier chapters along the horizontal axis from politically impossible to politically more feasible. Why consider the impossible at all? Because doing so will help to clarify what a genuine antidote to the presidential experience would entail—what it would take to remove or defuse the exposures. Of course, one reason such reforms are viewed as politically unacceptable is because they would surely give rise to operational problems of their own, problems that might prove to be worse than those they were intended to solve. Still, they can help sharpen our appreciation for how the presidential experience works. Further, the spirit of policy analysis—a perspective that seems appropriate here—requires some attention to the *range* of options, things capable of making a difference, not just things likely to be acceptable to majority opinion.

REMOVE FUNCTIONS

Thus we see that the first option, removing one or more of the functions now performed by the president, would simultaneously eliminate the exposures its performance entails. If the president were not responsible for mediation or crisis management, for exam-

Table 6 Reform Options

	Remove Functions	Install Plural Presidency	Change Citizen Attitudes	Legislative Question period and Censure motion
Stress	No crisis management no mediation no stress	Shared burdens	No impact	Increased stress
Deference	No symbol no deference	True peers	Wary disrespect	Counterbalance deference
Dissonance	No symbol no advocate no lying	Reduced discretion, peer surveillance	Vigilant skepticism	Discourage lying
Frustration	No advocacy no aggression	Depersonalized conflict increased restraint	Revised standards of presidential greatness	Increased frustration

ple, there would be considerably less stress. If the president were relieved of his duties as symbol of the republic, his exposure to deference would be greatly reduced. If he were neither symbol nor policy advocate, he would experience less pressure to create images of himself and his plans, and perhaps less temptation to fall back on deceit as a political resource. And a president stripped of his responsibilities for policy advocacy would rarely be thwarted, and just as rarely would he experience the frustrated anger that usually follows.

It is interesting to note that at least two of these radical changes have occasionally been taken seriously. The idea of detaching the symbolic function from the central executive, as the British Monarch is separate from the Prime Minister, has surfaced periodically as a part of proposals that the United States adopt a Cabinet form of government analogous to the British system. And the notion that policy advocacy is primarily the responsibility of the legislature and not the president has long been a tenet of strict constructionist interpretations of the Constitution, and of Madisonian visions of the presidency. Neither idea has created much real momentum, however; in the first instance because of the special rapport between the symbolic presidency and the people, and in the second because of the historic inability of the Congress to create the disciplined procedures or the unanimity required for policy control. Nor can we expect support for relocation of the mediation or crisis management functions to emerge, for no existing institution can rival the presidency in these areas, and there is little discernible sentiment in support of creating new national institutions.

Mention was made in an earlier chapter of the possibility of reducing the stressfulness of the president's workload by reassigning certain policy activities away from the White House, notably responsibility for policy implementation and evaluation. But it was noted that while this could reduce the sheer quantitative workload, it would do little to reduce the feeling of responsibility which is the origin of psychological stress. Taken as a whole, then, the prospect of diluting the presidential experience by removing the responsibilities that create it, although a seductively simple and effective solution, is so far removed from practical politics as to be impossible to implement.

A PLURAL PRESIDENCY

The prospects for a plural presidency, the next major option, are equally remote. But reflection on how a group would help is instructive, for it clarifies the great extent to which the problems described in this book arise from our reliance on the slender reed of a solitary, self-interested, and vulnerable human being. How and why could a group of, say, five co-equal presidents hope to escape that which touches and influences a lone ego?

As regards stress, the principal disadvantage of an individual rests with his personal vulnerability, whereas the main advantage of a group resides in the collectivization of responsibility. Stress would continue to beset a group. There would be no reason to expect any lessening of the workflow or any change in its qualitative nature. Demands would remain substantially the same, as would exposures. The differences would be in the cumulative psychological impact of stress upon a group as against an individual, and in the behavior of a stressed group versus a stressed individual.

Stress is threatening to a solitary president because it holds the very real prospect of failure—to achieve his aims and to meet the expectations of important others. This is what leads him to mobilize his energies and to burn them at a rate that works against their replenishment. And this is what leads him to isolate himself in search of relief from unceasing public attributions of responsibility.

Substitution of a group could create a psychological climate of increased safety, lessened individual vulnerability, and greater personal security among the participants. These things would foster increased objectivity and greater dispassion in dealing with problems than can be the case when the president is alone and there is no place to hide. Such are the comforts of human interaction that precisely comparable stresses feel much less onerous to an individual surrounded by peers in the same boat than when endured alone (Schacter, 1959). By increasing psychological comfort and promoting greater objectivity, a group would facilitate undistorted access to the available fund of human talent. Energies could be applied to the problem at hand rather than being diverted to anxiety management and self-protection. And there would be more energy to apply—the pool of nerve, ideas, surveillance potential, and cognitive power would be multipled. Under such an arrangement, we might expect a less permanent psychological impact to result from chronic stress, and a decreased incidence of such stress-induced behavior as emotional instability or physical deterioration. Also, a group with appropriate procedures could probably make better decisions than any single individual, working alone (Janis, 1972).

How would a group work against the distortions of deference? By giving the president true peers. If status equality characterized the relations among the members, the social comparison processes described in Chapter 4 would be reintroduced. In the absence of sycophancy as an information filter, the social and political ties of each co-president would serve to multiply the sources of information, interpretation, and opinion about important issues and events. Perceptual objectivity and accuracy might thus be increased. The chances for any systematic distortion in the group's collective perception would be significantly lessened in comparison with a solitary president. The incidence of such dangerous presidential behavior as overidentification or misinformed decisions might decline accordingly.

A group might also serve to check the limitless personal discretion that now enables solitary presidents to lie at will. A collection of presidential peers would introduce the normal social constraints on lying that tend to operate in human groups (Wright, 1971). A group might still decide that misrepresentation is a necessary and proper course. But the need for unanimity (a dissenter could simply leak the secret) would preclude much impulsive, face-saving misrepresentation as well as other causal or capricious uses of the resource. The inevitable discussion and debate of the options that would take place inside a group would make it difficult for group self-deception to flourish. In short, it would be harder for a group of presidents to lie to us for any reason.

Last, important differences could be expected in the responses of a group and a solitary president to frustration. The personalized struggles between presidents and rival power centers—Jackson and the Bank of the United States, Wilson and the Senate, Teddy

Roosevelt and the Trusts, FDR and the Court, JFK and Big Steel—would occur no more. This is not to suggest that a group would be free of conflict, or that other power centers would no longer seek to thwart a plural executive. Nor do I mean to imply that a collective presidency would not experience frustration. My point is simply that a plural presidency would depersonalize such conflict as did occur. A group would remove the potential for ego-involvement on the part of a solitary president, which is at the heart of the rigidification process that Barber (1977) attributes to his active-negative character type. Inside a group, conflict would be less likely to be felt and expressed in the bitter, personalized, vindictive manner of the threatened lone ego, determined to prevail at any cost. Where a solitary president tends to interpret opposition as a personal affront, a collective could achieve a much greater measure of emotional detachment. And though any member of a group presidency might get just as mad as have solitary presidents at the effronteries of opponents, still he would be vastly less free to act upon his passions. For none could decide alone. The need for consensus would thus reduce the likelihood of any impulsive executive action, and would increase the chances that democratic norms of restraint would receive a full hearing as they pertained to contemplated courses of action. For these reasons, we might expect less of a cumulative psychological impact upon a group from repeated exposure to frustration, and fewer instances of self-indulgent executive aggression.

From this brief review, it appears that a plural presidency would be substantially immune to the darker influence of the presidential experience. Such may indeed be the case, but the impression must not be left that a group would be entirely free of significant problems of its own. Though a group does look better on paper, it is an open question whether it could perform as effectively as has the traditional president. International experience is mixed. Switzerland's collective executive has performed well, while others, such as Uruguay's, have functioned poorly (Fitzgibbon, 1952). What might happen in the United States, with its unique political culture, is anybody's guess. Further, groups are subject to various pathologies of their own, such as groupthink (Janis, 1972) and the "risky-shift" phenomenon (Kelley and Thibaut, 1969). These could prove to be as dangerous to political stability as is the presidential experience. In any case, these uncertain consequences, plus the considerable risks that would accompany massive political change at this late date in the nation's history, effectively preclude the possibility of an experiment in pluralized executive leadership. Like removing presidential functions, installing a group is an alluring idea, but one that is quite unlikely to escape the drawing boards.

CITIZEN ATTITUDES

Next, we move a bit closer to the realm of the politically acceptable, but not that much closer to the realm of the practically possible. For few would contend that trying to change citizen attitudes and expectations is too radical a notion to win acceptance. The difficulty here is finding ways to implant, and most particularly to sustain, new public attitudes toward the presidency. But despite this problem, a sharp change in the nature and intensity of citizen feelings could supply at least a temporary antidote to the presidential experience. As was noted in the chapters describing each, deference might be mitigated by a wary disrespect on the part of citizens, dissonance by an aggressively vigilant citizen skepticism, and frustration by changes in accepted standards of presidential greatness and prevailing images of presidential potency.

We know now that our customary pattern of exaggerated respect for the office encourages presidents to conceive of their relation to the people in terms analogous to a parent dealing with children. Indeed, more than one president has used the parent-child metaphor to characterize his feelings for the great masses of Americans. Parents, of course, are concerned that their children love and respect them. But parents, in the natural course of things, feel free to ignore the advice of their children—feel free to act upon the assumption that "father knows best"—secure in the expectation that father's wisdom will be respected and obeyed, whether child happens to like it or not.

What if we were to turn suddenly skeptical and hostile to our elected "fathers?" What if the next generation was taught to assume that father will abuse and misuse us unless we watch him like a hawk? What if, instead of automatically respecting father, we cultivated a new generation with a skeptical, "show me" attitude? To abandon the metaphor, why couldn't we learn to treat our presidents the way the Canadians, Israelis, and British treat their prime ministers—with studied, occasionally belligerent disrespect?

My point is that if we established—in schools, families, and elsewhere—norms of suspicion and wariness toward the presidency as an institution and toward the president as a person, it would surely alter the incentive system and the influential exposures that presidents now confront. If citizens were taught to look upon the presidency as a necessary and useful, but potentially dangerous social machine, if they were encouraged to adopt a supervisory rather than a subservient attitude toward government, and if such views were to become proudly displayed symbols of the uniqueness of our political culture, then the problems associated with deference would be substantially reduced.

Under conditions like these, a president's mind set as he confronts the choices, chances, temptations, and frustrations would be markedly different. Particularly if citizen skepticism were reinforced by a movement away from all forms of ceremonial pomp and circumstance and all celebrations of the president's stature, he would feel obliged to regard himself as nothing more than the "first citizen"—a person who would think, and then think again before risking the use of deceit, however noble and worthy the ends to be served.

In order to discourage aggression, the new citizen vigilance would have to be supplemented by "revisionist" models of the presidency, and revisionist judgments of the performance of presidents past. Historians routinely acknowledge that history is, and must be, continuously rewritten as perceptions and evaluations of the past change in the light of new experience. Heretofore, our national experience has been cause for the idealization of the kind of dominant, assertive presidency epitomized by FDR and the aggressive giants of the past. And the polls of historians have reflected this fact. But after the sobering events of Vietnam and Watergate, it appears that new criteria for judging presidential performance—tailored more to such long-term survival values as a president's "fit" with his times, the wisdom and judiciousness displayed in his use of power, or the temperance and forbearance he displayed when angered or frustrated—might successfully compete with the old.

The new criteria would appropriately reflect certain tenets of behavioral science employed in this and other recent analyses of the presidency. These include appreciation for the fact that public expectations and routine work exposures tend, by their influence on presidents, to select some kinds of presidential behavior, and to extinguish other kinds. If the behavior now selected is too often dangerous, then the expectations and exposures that select it must be altered. The revised conceptions of presidential greatness likely to emerge would anoint some new heroes from the past and disenfranchise certain old heroes. Thus, for example, the behavior of presidents like Andrew Jackson or Teddy Roosevelt would probably come to seem destructive and inflammatory, whereas the quiet, colorless competence of men like Eisenhower or Cleveland would be accorded new respect.

There are some signs that our shared conceptions of the presidency are evolving. Jimmy Carter—the incumbent at this writing —revealed his sensitivity to these changes by de-emphasizing all symbolic vestiges of the imperial presidency, stressing trust and openness in government and making himself readily available to citizens and press alike. Near the close of his first year in office, 78% of 1,050 registered voters queried by the opinion research firm of Yankelovich, Skelly and White, felt Carter had made a "good start" at providing moral leadership. Seventy-six percent praised Carter for "having an open administration," and 65% said he made Americans "feel good."[6]

Another sign is to be found in the content of university courses now being offered on the presidency. Students in the 1960s read books like Clinton Rossiter's classic, *The American Presidency* (1960), or Neustadt's equally classic *Presidential Power* (1960), both of which hailed an assertive presidency as an innately positive force. Neustadt argued that what is good for the president is good for the country, while Rossiter enjoined Americans to leave the presidency alone. Nowadays, students read from a pool of critical, revisionist literature, like Tugwell and Cronin's *The Presidency Reappraised* (1974), Schlesinger's *The Imperial Presidency* (1973) or Cronin's *The State of the Presidency* (1975), and listen to lectures which call the assumptions about the benevolence and desirability of a powerful, activist presidency into serious question.

Have these changes in mood and expectations yet produced any concomitant changes in the presidential experience? This, of course, is the acid test for this particular reform. But based on the early indications—press analyses of the inner workings of the Carter administration—there have not been many changes. The indications were that Carter was trying to carry an excessive workload, that he was surrounded by an inexperienced "Georgia Mafia" of questionable competence and savvy who tended to defer to his judgment and to offer low-quality advice, that Carter had already indulged in at least one instance of politically inspired misrepresentation, and that he was frustrated by the unresponsiveness of Congress and by the impatient proddings of such disgruntled Democrats as labor and blacks. In response to the frequently encountered observation that he was aging visibly, Carter retorted that he "liked" living in Washington, and continued to "enjoy" his job. Though no evidence of imminent danger or trouble was apparent, it did seem clear that one year into the Carter presidency the forces of influence described in these pages remained busily at work. To that point at least, changed expectations had not yet markedly altered the presidential experience.

These things suggest that there are limits to what can be expected from attempts to alter citizen expectations or increase their vigilance. Not only is their impact uncertain, they are also inevitably impermanent. The sharp edge of concern spawned by Watergate has already ebbed away. The author of another recent book on the presidency, Erwin C. Hargrove (1974), argues persuasively that revisionist views of the presidency are bound to be short-lived because of the nature of our politics, and because future circumstances will inevitably give rise to renewed cries for heroic and assertive presidents. Thus, reliance on a watchful citizenry, informed by scaled-down visions of the presidency, seems inadequate as a long-term remedy for the presidential experience.

LEGISLATIVE REMEDIES

One last reform category external to the president deserves mention. Though more realistic, in political terms, than removing functions, installing a plural presidency, or resocializing citizens, it is still strong medicine. These "legislative remedies," as I call them, include two specific practices often encountered in parliamentary forms of government: the question period, and the censure motion. Both devices would fit the prevailing mood of Congressional reassertion (Dodd and Oppenheimer, 1977). Yet both would be politically and organizationally difficult to establish. Leaving these problems of implementation conveniently aside, let us confine our attention here to the question at hand: How would each help to counter the effects of the presidential experience?

A question period—a regularly scheduled event at which the president was required to answer personally questions posed by members of the Congress—would force the president to expose himself in a setting he did not control. Unlike the easily manipulated and usually sanitized press conference, this holds the prospect of being a humbling and difficult experience involving unprecedented symbolic subordination for any American president. Though in quiet times the questioning might be perfunctory, in anxious or contentious times it would undoubtedly become hostile and disrespectful. Americans would be treated to the spectacle of their highest officer submitting to suspicious, critical cross-examination, like any sworn witness on the stand facing an adversary attorney. It might at first be a shocking sight. Yet much could be gained if the president were forced to confront skeptical critics, at liberty to exclaim, "I beseech you, in the bowels of Christ, think it possible that you may be mistaken!" (Jennings, 1942, p. 77).

There can be little doubt that such an exposure would add markedly to the psychological stress experienced by presidents. And a like increment in frustration might result as well. Yet for this price important antidotes to deference and dissonance might be had. To the reflexive celebrations of his usual face-to-face encounters would be added the sobering, regularly scheduled assurance that his personal accountability would be unavoidable and swift. He would have no power to select his inquisitors, or to ignore their questions—though on sensitive matters closed sessions might be arranged. He could not count on gentle or respectful treatment; his station would afford him no cushioning. The questions would educate him as to the concerns that shape the thinking of those outside his protected circle. Whatever scorn or negativity he encountered might serve as a barometer of the sentiment his policies had inspired in his countrymen. In sum, a question period would be a sobering, chastening, and educational experience for a president. It would supply a forceful intrusion of reality into his deliberations. And it could serve as a strong antidote for any misperceptions that had taken root inside the White House.

The temptation to deceive would be leavened by the certain knowledge that all forms of embarrassing questions would be asked at the next encounter with the Congressmen—questions that must be answered under oath. The chances for discovery—plus accompanying embarrassment or censure—would increase. An accomplished presidential actor might lie anyway, but most would be discouraged from reliance on misrepresentation as a resource. Had Lyndon Johnson or Richard Nixon faced such regularly scheduled grillings, it seems likely that they would have looked beyond secrecy for solutions to Vietnam and Watergate.

Similarly, a censure motion, wherein a simple majority of both houses of Congress passed a resolution condemning presidential misbehaviors deemed insufficiently weighty for impeachment, could do much to muster and focus the vigilant attention of the country upon an unruly president. True, such a motion would carry none but symbolic punishment. But this could increase its chances for adoption. A censure motion represents no extreme change in power or procedure of the sort that discourages political support. But would such a motion accomplish anything? If a president knew the Congress had this additional arrow in its quiver, he might be less inclined to act on pique and more inclined to resist his own aggressive impulses. The reason is that a censure motion would put the public on its guard and threaten the president's ability to rally their support. It might thus serve as a silent caution against aggressive responses to frustration. Also, as the symbolic opposite of deference, its mere existence could help to counterbalance the effects of that exposure as well. Behind the ubiquitous reminders of his celebrated stature would lurk the knowledge that his acts as president could win him, if he strayed too far from democratic propriety or political reality, the public brand of liar, fool, or despot in the judgment of Congress.

As with all reform possibilities, there are drawbacks here as well. The opportunities for political abuse of these Congressional devices would be plentiful. They might be misapplied or used unfairly. Also, the question period would raise and force the resolution of the hotly contested issue of executive privilege. Some fear that denying this privilege and forcing presidents to submit themselves to Congress in this manner would alter too radically the pattern of competitive coexistence between the branches. The end result might be to blunt presidential power too well.

To this and other reservations about the reforms discussed here, I can only acknowledge that yes, each has a significant risk potential of its own. But the risks associated with the presidential experience seem to me to require strong measures to reduce. No reform capable of making a difference can possibly be free of either risk or the potential for major controversy.

RÉSUMÉ

These, in brief, are the four classes of reform that seem to me to offer the best hope for genuine modifications of the presidential experience. Though they vary from unthinkably radical to just barely plausible in political terms, none is likely of adoption in the present climate. For all would introduce disruptions with uncertain consequences for the status quo—disruptions that won't be risked without absolutely compelling circumstances or immediately urgent incentives. The value of considering unlikely reform options at all comes down to having a list of possibilities at hand should the presidential experience give rise to future trouble and rekindle the thirst for reform—things which are all too likely to happen.

The reason is—to recapitulate the central argument of this book—that presidents are socialized in ways that can lead any president to behave in aggressive, deceitful, or incompetent ways. Not all succumb, of course. And some—like active-positives or Eisenhower-like moderate character types—do a better job than others of staying on equal terms with the pressures. But all are human, and humans tend to respond to recurring influence in spite of themselves.

In the absence of any hope for significant reform, the only remaining option is to extend and refine, along the lines suggested by Barber (1977), our ability to gauge character. In this effort, a systematic sense of what the presidency does to presidents—how it uses and abuses them in recurring and important ways—can be helpful. I hope this book moves us closer to such an understanding.

NOTES

1. On the history of the presidency, see Wilfred E. Binkley, *President and Congress* (1962); James MacGregor Burns, *Presidential Government* (1965); and Rexford G. Tugwell, *The Enlargement of the Presidency* (1960). Works with briefer but still useful sections on presidential history include Edward S. Corwin, *The President: Office and Powers 1787–1957* (1957); Harold J. Laski, *The American Presidency* (1940); and Herman Finer, *The Presidency: Crisis and Regeneration* (1960).

2. I share the view of numerous political theorists who assert that the first purpose of government is to establish and preserve social order and

physical safety for its citizens. When the political stability that underlies order is threatened, protecting it takes temporal precedence over
concern for democracy or for executive effectiveness.

3. Whether or not the president should be conceived of as a "manager"
has been a popular question lately. Stephen Hess, for example, argues
that when presidents try to "manage" programs or the bureaucracy,
they wind up spending too much time doing what others could do as
well, and less time on matters only they can handle. See Hess's *Organizing the Presidency* (1976). For a similar view, see Rose's article,
"The President: A Chief but Not An Executive" (1977). Contrary
views are expressed by Donald Haider (1976) and Thomas Cronin
(1975).

4. Bruce Miroff, in his book, *Pragmatic Illusions: The Presidential Politics of John F. Kennedy* (1976, p. 294), implicitly scolds the presidency for its failure to seek acceptance for a program of social and
economic reconstruction, and for its service to established power and
established values, arguing that "even the most liberal presidents have
done far more to preserve existing patterns of power and wealth than to
alter them."

5. My use of words like "self-indulgence" and "breast-thumping" is an
expression of my belief that when the primary discernible motive behind an act of presidential assertiveness is personal—that is, aimed at
assuring the greater glory of the president involved as much or more
than at advancing the values of the United States as a whole—such a
motive constitutes an unacceptable threat to political stability. Obviously, the historical record of presidential assertiveness—especially
the motives behind specific instances of presidential aggression—is
subject to varying interpretation. The reader is invited to examine such
instances and to decide for himself.

6. Reported in *Time Magazine*, December 26, 1977, pp. 10–12.

Adams, H. (1918). *The Education of Henry Adams*. Boston: Massachusetts Historical Society.

Adams, J. W. (1826). *Diary*. December 7. Quoted in R. G. Tugwell (1960) *The Enlargement of the Presidency*. Garden City, New York: Doubleday, p. 83.

Alderfer, C. P. and L. D. Brown. (1975). *Learning from Changing: Organizational Diagnosis and Development*. Beverly Hills: Sage Library of Social Research, Volume 19.

Alker, H. A. (1976). "Presidential Lying." Paper presented at the *84th Annual Meeting, American Psychological Association*, Washington, D.C.

American Heritage Pictorial History of the Presidents. (1968). "Franklin Delano Roosevelt." New York: American Heritage Publishing Company Inc., p. 805.

Aronson, E. (1972). *The Social Animal*. San Francisco: W. H. Freeman.

———and D. R. Mettee. (1968). "Dishonest Behavior as a Function of Different Levels of Induced Self-Esteem." *Journal of Personality and Social Psychology*, 9:173–185.

Bailey, T. A. (1966). *Presidential Greatness*. New York: Appleton-Century-Crofts.

Barber, J. D. (1977a). *The Presidential Character: Predicting Performance in the White House*, Second Edition. Englewood Cliffs: Prentice-Hall, Inc.

———. (1977b). "Comment: Quall's Nonsensical Analysis of Nonexistent Works." *American Political Science Review* 71:212–225.

———. (1972). *The Presidential Character: Predicting Performance in the White House*. Englewood Cliffs: Prentice Hall, Inc.

———. (1965). *The Lawmakers: Recruitment and Adaptation To Legislative Life*. New Haven: Yale.

References

Barker, R. G. (1965). "Explorations in Ecological Psychology." *American Psychologist* 20:1–14.

――――. and H. F. Wright (1955). *Midwest and Its Children*. New York: Harper and Row.

Barnard, C. I. (1938). *The Functions of the Executive*. Cambridge: Harvard.

Basowitz, H., H. Persky, S. Korchin, and R. Grinker (1955). *Anxiety and Stress*. New York: McGraw-Hill.

Berger, P. L. and T. Luckman (1967). *The Social Construction of Reality*. Garden City, New York: Doubleday.

Binkley, W. E. (1962). *President and Congress*. Third Edition. New York: Vintage Books.

――――. (1958). *The Man in the White House*. Revised Edition. New York: Harper and Row.

Blum, J. M. (1972). *Roosevelt and Morgenthau*. Boston: Houghton Mifflin.

Bourne, P. G. (1971). "Altered Adrenal Function in Two Combat Situations in Viet Nam." In B. E. Eleftheriou and J. P. Scott (eds.), *The Physiology of Aggression and Defeat*. New York: Plenum, pp. 265–305.

Branden, N. (1971). *The Psychology of Self-Esteem*. New York: Bantam.

Brodie, F. M. (1974). *Thomas Jefferson: An Intimate History*. New York: Norton.

Browning, R. P. and H. Jacob (1964). "Power Motivation and the Political Personality." *Public Opinion Quarterly* 28:75–90.

Burns, J. M. (1965). *Presidential Government: The Crucible of Leadership*. Boston: Houghton Mifflin.

Carter, J. (1975). *Why Not the Best?* Nashville: Broadman Press.

Child, J. L. and I. K. Waterhouse (1953). "Frustration and the Quality of Performance." *Psychological Review* 60:127–139.

Clinch, N. G. (1973). *The Kennedy Neurosis*. New York: Grosset and Dunlap.

Cohen, A. R. (1959). "Some Implications of Self-Esteem for Social Influence." In C. I. Hovland and I. L. Janis (eds.), *Personality and Persuasibility*. New Haven: Yale.

Cohen, B. V. (1974). "Presidential Responsibility and American Democracy." 1974 Royer Lecture, University of California, Berkeley, May 23.

Cole, C., E. R. Oetting, and J. Hinkle (1967). "Non-Linearity of Self Concept Discrepancy—The Value Dimension." *Psychological Reports* 21: 58–60.

Coleman, J. C. (1960). *Personality Dynamics and Effective Behavior.* Chicago: Scott Foresman.

Corwin, E. S. (1957). *The President: Office and Powers 1787–1957.* New York: New York University Press.

Costello, T. W. and S. S. Zalkind (1963). *Psychology in Administration: A Research Orientation.* Englewood Cliffs: Prentice-Hall.

Coyle, D. C. (1960). *The Ordeal of the Presidency.* Washington, D. C.: Public Affairs Press.

Cronin, T. E. (1975). *The State of the Presidency.* Boston: Little, Brown.

Cunliffe, M. (1972). *American Presidents and the Presidency.* New York: American Heritage Press.

Dean, J. W. (1976). *Blind Ambition.* New York: Simon and Schuster.

de Grazia, A. (1969). "The Myth of the President." In A. Wildavsky (ed.), *The Presidency.* Boston: Little Brown.

Di Renzo, G. J. (1974). *Personality and Politics.* Garden City, New York: Doubleday.

Dodd, L. C. and B. I. Oppenheimer (1977). *Congress Reconsidered.* New York: Praeger.

Easton, D. (1965). *A Systems Analysis of Political Life.* New York: Wiley.

Eisenhower, D. D. (1965). *Waging Peace: 1956–1961.* Garden City, New York: Doubleday.

Erickson, E. H. (1968). *Identity: Youth and Crisis.* New York: W. W. Norton.

Fenno, R. (1959). *The President's Cabinet.* Cambridge: Harvard.

Festinger, L. (1957). *A Theory of Cognitive Dissonance.* Palo Alto: Stanford.

⸻. (1954). "Motivations Leading to Social Behavior." In M. R. Jones (ed.), *Nebraska Symposium on Motivation.* Lincoln: University of Nebraska, pp. 191–219.

Finer, H. (1960). *The Presidency: Crisis and Regeneration.* Chicago: University of Chicago.

Fitch, G. (1970). "Effects of Self-Esteem, Perceived Performance, and

Choice on Causal Attributions." *Journal of Personality and Social Psychology* 16: 311–315.

Fitzgibbon, R. H. (1952). "Adoption of a Collegiate Executive in Uruguay." *Journal of Politics* 14:616–642.

Flexner, James T. (1970). *George Washington and the New Nation.* Boston: Little, Brown.

George, A. L. (1975). "Psychological Aspects of Decision-Making: Adapting to Constraints on Rational Decision-Making." In Volume 2, Appendix D: *Commission on the Organization of the Government for the Conduct of Foreign Policy.* Washington, D.C.: Government Printing Office, pp. 17–29.

———. (1974). "Assessing Presidential Character." *World Politics* 26:234–282.

———. (1972). "The Case for Multiple Advocacy in Making Foreign Policy." *American Political Science Review* 66:751–785.

———. (1969). "The 'Operational Code': A Neglected Approach to the Study of Political Leaders and Decision-Making." *International Studies Quarterly* 13:190–222.

——— and J. L. George (1956). *Woodrow Wilson and Colonel House*: A Personality Study. New York: Dover Publications.

Gordon, C. and K. J. Gergen, eds. (1968). *The Self in Social Interaction.* Volume 1. New York: Wiley.

Graf, R. (1971). "Induced Self-Esteem as a Determinant of Behavior." *Journal of Social Psychology* 85:213–217.

Greenstein, F. I. (1975). "Personality and Politics." In F. I. Greenstein and N. W. Polsby (eds.), *Handbook of Political Science.* Volume 3, Micropolitics. Reading, Mass: Addison-Wesley, pp. 1–91.

———. (1974). "What the President Means to Americans." In J. D. Barber (ed.), *Choosing the President.* Englewood Cliffs: Prentice-Hall, Inc., pp. 121–147.

———. (1973). "Political Psychology: A Pluralistic Universe." In J. N. Knudson (ed.), *Handbook of Political Psychology.* San Francisco: Jossey-Bass.

———. (1969). *Personality and Politics: Problems of Evidence, Inference, and Conceptualization.* Chicago: Markham.

Haider, D. (1976). "Management and the Presidency: From Preparation to Performance." *Presidential Studies Quarterly* 6:4–15.

Hall, C. S. (1954). *A Primer of Freudian Psychology*. Cleveland: World Publishing.

———— and G. Lindzey (eds.) (1970). *Theories of Personality*. Second edition. New York: John Wiley.

Hargrove, E. C. (1974). *The Power of the Modern Presidency*. New York: Knopf.

————. (1966). *Presidential Leadership: Personality and Political Style*. Toronto: Collier-Macmillan.

Hermann, M. G. and C. F. Hermann (1975). "Maintaining the Quality of Decision-Making in Foreign Policy Crises: A Proposal." In Volume 2, Appendix D: *Commission on the Organization of the Government for the Conduct of Foreign Policy*. Washington, D.C.: Government Printing Office, pp. 124–136.

Hess, S. (1976). *Organizing the Presidency:* Washington, D. C.: Brookings.

————. (1974). *The Presidential Campaign*. Washington, D.C.: Brookings.

Hofstadter, R. (1948). *The American Political Tradition*. New York: Random House.

Hughes, E. J. (1972). *The Living Presidency*. New York: Coward, McCann and Geoghegan.

Hummel, R. P. (1977). *The Bureaucratic Experience*. New York: St. Martin's.

Huntington, S. P. (1968). *Political Order in Changing Societies*. New Haven: Yale.

Inkeles, A. and D. J. Levinson (1971). "The Personal System and the Socio-cultural System in Large-Scale Organizations." In F. I. Greenstein and Michael Lerner (eds.), *A Source Book for the Study of Personality and Politics*. Chicago: Markham.

Janis, I. L. (1972). *Victims of Groupthink*. Boston: Houghton Mifflin.

———— and H. Leventhal (1968). "Human Reactions to Stress." In E. F. Borgatta and W. W. Lambert (eds.), *Handbook of Personality Theory and Research*. Chicago: Rand McNally, pp. 1041–1085.

———— and L. Mann (1977). *Decision-Making: A Psychological Analysis of Conflict, Choice, and Commitment*. New York: Free Press.

Jennings, W. I. (1942). *The British Constitution*. Cambridge: Cambridge University Press.

Johnson, L. B. (1971). *The Vantage Point: Perspectives of the Presidency 1963–1969*. New York: Popular Library.

Johnson, R. T. (1974). *Managing the White House*. New York: Harper and Row.

Kallenbach, J. H. (1971). "The Presidency and the Constitution: A Look Ahead." In N. C. Thomas and H. W. Baadle (eds.), *The Institutionalized Presidency*. Dobbs Ferry, New York: Oceana Publications.

Katz, D. (1963). "Determinants of Attitude Arousal and Attitude Change." In T. W. Costello and S. S. Zalkind (eds.), *Psychology in Administration*. Englewood Cliffs: Prentice-Hall, Inc., pp. 265–276.

_____ and R. L. Kahn (1966). *The Social Psychology of Organizations*. New York: Wiley.

Kearns, D. (1976). *Lyndon Johnson and the American Dream*. New York: Harper and Row.

Kelley, H. H. and J. W. Thibaut (1969). "Group Problem Solving." In G. Lindzey and E. Aronson (eds.), *The Handbook of Social Psychology*. Second Edition, Volume 4. Reading, Mass.: Addison-Wesley, pp. 1–101.

Kiesler, C. A., (1971). *The Psychology of Commitment*. New York: Academic Press.

Koenig, L. W. (1975). *The Chief Executive*. Third edition. New York: Harcourt Brace.

Lacey, J. I. (1959). "Psychophysiological Approaches to the Evaluation of Psychotherapeutic Process and Outcome." In E. A. Rubinstein and M. B. Parloff (eds.), *Research in Psychotherapy*. Washington, D.C.: American Psychological Association, pp. 160–208.

Lammers, W. W. (1976). *Presidential Politics: Patterns and Prospects:* New York: Harper and Row.

Laski, H. J. (1940). *The American Presidency: An Interpretation*. New York: Grosset and Dunlap.

Lasswell, H. D. (1951). *The Political Writings of Harold D. Lasswell*. New York: Free Press.

Lazarus, R. S. (1966). *Psychological Stress and the Coping Process*. New York: McGraw-Hill.

Levinson, D. J. (1971). "Role, Personality, and Social Structure in the Organizational Setting." In F. I. Greenstein and M. Lerner (eds.), *A Source Book for the Study of Personality and Politics*. Chicago: Markham, pp. 61–74.

Lewin, K. (1936). "Psychology of Success and Failure." *Occupations* 14: 926–930.

Loss, R. (1976). "Dissolving Concepts of the Presidency: Four Reviews." *Presidential Studies Quarterly* 6:64–83.

Lurie, L. (1972). *The Running of Richard Nixon*. New York: Coward, McCann and Geoghegan.

Mabel, S. and H. M. Rosenfeld (1966). "Relationship of Self-Concept to the Experience of Imbalance in P-O-X Situations." *Human Relations* 19: 381–389.

MacRae, D. (1976). *The Social Function of Social Sciences*. New Haven: Yale.

Malone, D. (1970). *Jefferson the President: First Term 1801–1805*. Boston: Little, Brown.

Mazlish, B. (1972). *In Search of Nixon*. New York: Basic Books.

McCandless, B. (1961). *Children and Adolescents: Behavior and Development*. New York: Holt, Rinehart and Winston.

McCloskey, R. G. (1960). *The American Supreme Court*. Chicago: University of Chicago.

McFarland, A. S. (1969). *Power and Leadership in Pluralist Systems*. Palo Alto: Stanford.

Miroff, B. (1976). *Pragmatic Illusions: The Presidential Politics of John F. Kennedy*. New York: McKay.

Mueller, J. E. (1973). *War, Presidents and Public Opinion*. New York: Wiley.

Neustadt, R. E. (1976). *Presidential Power: The Politics of Leadership, With Reflections on Johnson and Nixon*. New York: Wiley.

——. (1969). "The Presidency at Mid-Century." In A. Wildavsky (ed.), *The Presidency*. Boston: Little, Brown, pp. 193–229.

——. (1960). *Presidential Power*. New York: Wiley.

Oates, S. B. (1977). *With Malice Toward None: The Life of Abraham Lincoln*. New York: Harper and Row.

Pavlov, I. P. (1927). *Conditioned Reflexes* (trans. by G. V. Anrep). London: Oxford.

Phillips, C. (1966). *The Truman Presidency*. Baltimore: Penguin.

Plesur, M. (1974). "The Health of Presidents." In R. G. Tugwell and T.

E. Cronin (eds.), *The Presidency Reappraised*. New York: Praeger, pp. 187–204.

Pringle, H. R. (1956). *Theodore Roosevelt*. New York: Harcourt, Brace and World.

Qualls, J. H. (1977). "Barber's Typological Analysis of Political Leaders." *American Political Science Review* 71:182–211.

Radloff, R. (1968). "Affiliation and Social Comparison." In E. F. Borgatta and W. W. Lambert (eds.), *Handbook of Personality Theory and Research*. Chicago: Rand McNally, pp. 943–958.

Rather, D. and G. P. Gates (1974). *The Palace Guard*. New York: Harper and Row.

Reedy, G. E. (1973). *The Presidency in Flux*. New York: Columbia University.

———. (1970). *The Twilight of the Presidency*. New York: World.

Rogin, M. P. (1975). *Fathers and Children*. New York: Knopf.

Rogow, A. A. and H. D. Lasswell (1963). *Power, Corruption, and Rectitude*. Englewood Cliffs: Prentice-Hall, Inc.

Rokeach, M. (1973). *The Nature of Human Values*. New York: Free Press.

Rose, R. (1977). "The President: A Chief But Not an Executive." *Presidential Studies Quarterly* 7:5–20.

Rosenberg, M. J. (1965). "When Dissonance Fails: On Eliminating Evaluation Apprehension From Attitude Measurement." *Journal of Personality and Social Psychology* 1:28–42.

Roper, Burns (1968). "The Public Looks at Presidents: Thirty Years of Polls." *The Public Pulse* 28.

Rossiter, C. (1960). *The American Presidency*. Second edition. New York: Harcourt, Brace.

Safire, W. (1975). *Before the Fall*. Garden City, New York: Doubleday.

Schacter, S. (1959). *The Psychology of Affiliation*. Palo Alto: Stanford.

Schalon, C. (1968). "Effect of Self-Esteem Upon Performance Following Failure Stress." *Journal of Consulting and Clinical Psychology* 32:497.

Schlesinger, A. (1945). *The Age of Jackson*. Boston: Little, Brown.

———. (1965). *A Thousand Days: John F. Kennedy in the White House*. Boston: Houghton Mifflin.

———. (1973). *The Imperial Presidency*. Boston: Houghton Mifflin.

Schutz, A. (1967). "Common-Sense and Scientific Interpretation of Human Action." In *Collected Papers*, Volume 2. The Hague: Martinus Nijhoff.

Selznick, P. (1957). *Leadership in Administration*. New York: Harper and Row.

Sherwood, R. E. (1948). *Roosevelt and Hopkins: An Intimate History*. New York: Harper and Row.

Shoggen, P. (1963). "Environmental Forces in the Everyday Lives of Children." In R. G. Barker (ed.), *The Stream of Behavior*. New York: Appleton-Century-Crofts, pp. 42–69.

Shrauger, J. and S. Rosenberg (1970). "Self-Esteem and the Effects of Success and Failure Feedback on Performance." *Journal of Personality* 33:404–414.

Sidey, H. (1968). *A Very Personal Presidency: Lyndon Johnson in the White House*. New York: Atheneum.

Sigel, R. S. (1969). "Image of the American Presidency: Part II of an Exploration into Popular Views of Presidential Power." in A. Wildavsky (ed.), *The Presidency*. Boston: Little, Brown, pp. 296–309.

Simon, H. A. (1945). *Administrative Behavior*. Second edition. New York: Free Press.

Skinner, B. F. (1938). *The Behavior of Organisms*. New York: Appleton-Century-Crofts.

Small, N. J. (1932). "Some Presidential Interpretations of the Presidential Role." In *Johns Hopkins University Studies in Historical and Political Science,* 50:93–300.

Smith, M. B. (1973). "Political Attitudes." In J. N. Knutson, (ed.), *Handbook of Political Psychology*. San Francisco: Jossey-Bass, pp. 57–82.

Sniderman, P. M. (1975). *Personality and Democratic Politics*. Berkeley: University of California.

Sorensen, T. C. (1965). *Kennedy*. New York: Harper and Row.

Steinberg, A. (1968). *Sam Johnson's Boy*. New York: Macmillan.

Stokes, W. S. (1976). "Whig Conceptions of Executive Power." *Presidential Studies Quarterly* 6:16–35.

Stotland, E., S. Thorley, E. Thomas, A. Cohen, and A. Zander (1957).

"Group Expectations, Self-Esteem, and Self-Evaluations." *Journal of Abnormal and Social Psychology* 54:55–63.

Super, D. E., R. Starishevsky, N. Matlin, and J. P. Jordaan (1963). *Career Development: Self Concept Theory*. New York: College Entrance Examination Board.

Tiedeman, D. V. and R. P. O'Hara (1963). *Career Development: Choice and Adjustment*. New York: College Entrance Examination Board.

Torrance, E. P. (1963). "The Behavior of Small Groups Under the Stress of Survival." In T. W. Costello and S. S. Zalkind (eds.), *Psychology In Administration*. Englewood Cliffs: Prentice-Hall, Inc., pp. 128–129.

Truman, D. B. (1951). *The Governmental Process*. New York: Knopf.

Truman, H. S. (1955). *Memoirs by Harry S. Truman: Year of Decisions*. Garden City, New York: Doubleday.

———. (1956). *Memoirs by Harry S. Truman: Years of Trial and Hope*. Garden City, New York: Doubleday.

Tugwell, R. G. (1974). "On Bringing Presidents to Heel." In R. G. Tugwell and T. E. Cronin (eds.), *The Presidency Reappraised*. New York: Praeger, pp. 266–294.

———. (1960). *The Enlargement of the Presidency*. Garden City, New York: Doubleday.

——— and T. E. Cronin (eds.), (1974). *The Presidency Reappraised*. New York: Praeger.

Van Gennep, A. (1960). *The Rites of Passage*. Chicago: University of Chicago.

von Bertalanffy, L. (1968). *General System Theory*. New York: Braziller.

———. (1956). "General System Theory." *General Systems*. Yearbook of the Society for the Advancement of General System Theory 1:1–10.

Weinstein, E. A. (1967). "Denial of Presidential Disability: A Case Study of Woodrow Wilson." *Psychiatry* 30:376–391.

Wells, L. E. and G. Marwell (1976). *Self-Esteem: Its Conceptualization and Measurement*. Beverly Hills: Sage Library of Social Research, Volume 20.

White, T. H. (1975). *Breach of Faith*. New York: Atheneum.

Wills, G. (1969). *Nixon Agonistes*. Boston: Houghton Mifflin.

Wise, D. (1973). *The Politics of Lying: Government Deception, Secrecy and Power*. New York: Vintage.

Witkin, H. A., R. B. Dyk, H. F. Faterson, D. R. Goadenough, and S. A. Karp (1962). *Psychological Differentiation: Studies of Development*. New York: Wiley.

Wolkinson, H. (1949). "Demands of Congressional Committees for Executive Papers." *Federal Bar Journal* April, pp. 103, 105.

Woodward, B. and C. Bernstein (1976). *The Final Days*. New York: Simon and Schuster.

Wright, D. (1971). *The Psychology of Moral Behavior*. Baltimore: Penguin.

Wylie, R. C. (1974). *The Self Concept*. Volume 1. Revised Edition. Lincoln, Nebraska: University of Nebraska.

———. (1968). "The Present Status of Self Theory." In E. F. Borgatta and W. W. Lambert (eds.), *Handbook of Personality Theory and Research*. Chicago: Rand-McNally, pp. 728–787.

Young, J. S. (1966). *The Washington Community: 1800–1828*. New York: Columbia University.

Index

191